Divine Essence of Love

Spiritual Poetry

Open to any page for contemplation, insights, encouragement, and guidance.

Nancy Clark, Ph.D.

From the author of *Our Divinity Revealed, Master Plant Teachers,* and *Ascendance*

KNOW THYSELF AS DIVINITY

© 2024 Nancy Clark

All rights reserved. No part of this book may be reproduced or transmitted in any form or by any means without written permission of the publisher, except in the case of brief quotations embedded in critical articles, books, and reviews.

This material has been written and published solely for educational purposes. The author and the publisher shall have neither liability nor responsibility to any person or entity with respect to any loss, damage, or injury caused or alleged to be caused directly or indirectly by the information contained in this book.

The intent of the author is only to offer information of a general nature to help the reader in the quest for well-being. In the event the reader uses any of the information in this book of self or others, which is a constitutional right. The author and the publisher assume no responsibility for the actions of the reader.

Published by

Dr. Nancy Clark, Ph.D. Publishing | nancyclarkphd.com

Publisher's Cataloging-in-Publication Data

Clark, Nancy, Ph.D.

Divine essence of love : spiritual poetry / Nancy Clark, Ph.D. – Ormond Beach, FL : Dr. Nancy Clark, Ph.D. Pub., 2024.

p. ; cm.

ISBN13: 978-0-9601223-2-5 (Hardcover)

978-0-9601223-3-2 (Softcover)

1. Spiritual life--Poetry. I. Title.

PS3603.L37 D58

Project coordination by Jenkins Group, Inc. | www.jenkinsgroupinc.com

Printed in the United States of America

28 27 26 25 24 • 5 4 3 2 1

Dedication

To Divine Source, who goes by thousands of names.
The pathway to you is love.
You dance to the delight in many forms.
Creation is unique expressions of you.
Your Divine Essence is hidden within,
But wise are those who recognize you.
O Beloved, the recognition of Source within
Is those who are lost in your love.
We are together everywhere, like the wave and the ocean.

Contents

Acknowledgments — xi

Introduction — xiii

Poetry *Divine Outpouring of Source Energy* — 1

Divine Essence of Love	2
Divine Love Bliss	3
Inner Voice	4
Bliss of Oneness	5
Mystery of Life	6
Light and Darkness	7
Expression	8
Saturation	9
Happiness	10
Delight of Service	11
Song of Oneness	12
Seek and Find	13
Within All	14
Service to the Divine Plan	15
Expansion	16
Crystals	17
An Agreement	18
Love Spell	19
Homesick	20
Seagull	21
Mother Ayahuasca	24
Always More	25
Come Back Home	26
Infinite Journey	27
Pure Awareness	28
Choice	29
Challenges	30
Sound Current	31

Waking Dream	32
Spiritual Battle	33
Surrendered	34
Plateau	35
A Cry for Meaning	36
Sacrifice	37
Oneness with Source	38
Divinity	39
Profound Soul	40
Promises of Light	41
Story of You	42
Primordial Light	43
Higher Self and Lower Self	44
Love along the Journey	45
Highway of Love	46
Poetry is a Song	47
Enlightenment	48
Cosmic Drama	49
Incarnation	50
Dark Night of the Soul	51
Empowerment	52
Real Love	53
Brought Light into Darkness	54
Evolved	55
Light Warrior	56
World of the Ego	57
Transcendence	58
Between Life and Death	59
True Essence	60
Deep Connection	61
Light of Truth	62
Fathom the Splendor	63
Your Ship Has Come In	64
Ego's Web	65
Know Thyself As Divinity	66
Vastness inside of You	67
Abundance of Jubilation	68
Magnificent Journey	69
Spiritual Phone to Call Home	70

Spell of Illusion	71
Higher Viewpoint	72
Light Armor	73
Collective Neurosis	74
Quest for Meaning	75
Higher States of Being	76
Divine Shines through You	77
Descent into Darkness	78
Origins Unveiled	79
Rebirth of the Soul	80
Rise	81
Enchanted	82
Journey to Glory	83
Archangel	84
Road to Majesty	85
Pure Divine Love	86
Existence	87
Horizon of Light	88
Spirited Shift	89
Aurora	90
Victory	91
World of Dreams	92
Burden of a Blessing	93
Inner Light	94
Strength and Honor	95
Reminiscing Home	96
Higher Light Being	97
Spiritual Special Forces	98
Sacred Connection	99
Rise in Love	100
True Mastership	101
Divine Love Frequency	103
Beyond the Ego	104
Energetic Sovereignty	105
Grand Overall Design	106
Mastership Level	107
Deeper Degree	108
A Realized Soul	109
Excitement of Reuniting	110

Expansion	111
Remarkable	112
Exploration	113
Splendor	114
Celestial Essence	115
Majestic Power of Soul	116
Real from Unreal	117
Magnetic	118
Glorious	119
Walking Divinity	120
Temple of Light	121
Divine Dance	122
Tranquility	123
Divine Days	124
Ultimate Testing	125
Endurance	126
A Diamond	127
You and Source	128
Spiritual Progress is Earned	129
Spread This Light	130
Energy of Soul	131
Living Dead	132
Secret Garden	133
Life Force	134
Paradox	135
Light Ambassador	136
Walking Temple of Source	137
Love Potion	138
Soul and Beloved	139
Soul Vs. Mind	140
Becoming You	141
Purification	142
Next to You	143
Singing to You	144
Transcended	145
Your Gift	146
Oneness	147
Divine Union	148
Pierce the Veil	149

Duality	150
Sacrifice	151
Ocean of Tears	152
Courting with Delight	153
Destiny	154
Holding Hands	155
Run Quickly	156
Late-Night Date	157
Living Image	158
Sing to the Divine	159
Marked	160
Union with Sound	161
Wild Ride	162
Unforgettable	164
Higher Realm	165
Magnetic Attraction	166
Being in Love	167
Love Letter	168
Wearing Glasses	169
Love toward You	170
Secret Love Affair	171
Quietness	172
Do You Hear?	173
Conversation	174
Fresh Flowers	176
Medicine	177
Divine Elixir	178
Heartache	179
Gaia	180
Awakening	181
Pierced My Heart	182
Our Time	183
Awake!	184
Beloved is Waiting	185
Captivity	186
Crazy Love	187
Divine Love Call	188
Grace	189
Heart Sense	190

Drowning	191
Life Changes	192
Love Call	193
Love Has Come	194
Forever Together	195
Love Rays	196
Happiness	197
Outside Vs. Inside	198
Divine Laughter	199
Redirection	200
Sacred Brew	201
Lightworker	202
Assignment	203
Stars	204
Family of Light	205
Living Water	206
Celestial Music	207
Helplessly Mine	208
Dolphins	209
The Journey	210
Perfume	211
Reservoir	212
Tears of Joy	213
Inner Majesty	214
Snowflakes	215
Long for You	216
Watchful	217
Circus Show	218
Ascendance	219
Enchantment	220
Precious One	221
Beloved's Arrow	222
A Mystical Journey	223
You are the Violin	224

About the Author   225

Acknowledgments

I would like to thank Divine Source for this unique expression of life and the ability to serve the Divine Plan. I would like to express my gratitude to all the people who have come into my life who have reminded me of my true identity, without whom this book would not have been possible. So many teachers all had something to add and cause the remembrance, including the Master Plant Teacher, Mother Ayahuasca. I want to honor so many beautiful Souls who have walked along with me, some for a short while and others for much longer. I applaud you, brave Souls, for coming into this world to understand more deeply your true identity as a piece of Source by experiencing the illusion of separation.

Introduction

Why do you feel alone?
When have I told you
you are alone?

This feeling is fleeting,
comes and goes.
Can't you see me,
next to you,
looking into your eyes?

Beautiful one,
special one,
how can I ever
forget you?

You are made from
the essence of myself.

I loved you before
Heavens were created.

How can I forget myself?

Poetry

Divine Outpouring of Source Energy

Poems have come as an outpouring of Divine energy moving through me and as a form of expression into the world. This poetry book has all poems that have been created by me, the author. The poems are original and have been written over a course of many years and now have a place to be released out into the public to enjoy them.

Divine Essence of Love

Radiance Beyond Measure
Illumination of Love Sensation
Divine Essence creation of Souls
Reflection of Source in You

You are Cherished
You are a Treasure
Blaze your Luminosity
Shine like the Sun

Show your Brilliancy
You are a walking temple
Splendor of Light
Glow with Love Reflection

Delight in being Cherished
You are the Essence of Love
Conviction to serve the Light
Passion toward Divine Bliss

Euphoria of Rapture
Exuberance of Paradise
Joyousness of Nirvana
Jubilation of Love intoxication

You are made from Love
Divine Covenant to You
You are One with Divine Essence
A Divine Being in Form

Divine Love Bliss

Started my day
Talking with you
My head Euphoric
Divine Love Bliss

How can I get my work done?
You have me whirling with you
I hear the birds singing
Wind through the trees

I see you everywhere
Constantly reminded of you
Connection felt on the other side
Before I incarnated into form

My Heart Remembers
Our Union, Our Love
Divine Love Bliss
Joyous Connection

Words are unable to express
Magnitude of Love
Beloved has my heart
Separation is illusion

I hear your whispers
Divine Love Call
Feeling your inner warmth
I am here with you

Stepped into form to have expression
A sense of individuality
Only in physical realms
Full understanding of connection

Inner Voice

I hear your whispers
"You Are Loved"

Ride the wave
Celestial sound music
Life giving, Beloved's Voice
Get quiet enough

You can hear it
Beloved is always there
Watching, waiting, whispering
Turn your face away

From the world to retreat
Quiet time needed
Spend moments with this power
Guides your way onward

All of creation sings to you
Beloved is around you
Shines within you
Beautiful Brilliant Soul

Bliss of Oneness

Recognition of Divine Oneness
Causing the Bliss
Heart pierced with Love
How can one explain this knowingness

You are the Lighthouse in Human Form
Stay with the Divine Presence
Oneness with Divine Essence
Saturation of Love Waves

Unique expression in form
Source divided Itself
For physical experience
Returns back to Oneness

Feel that knowingness
Connect with your Divinity
Wisdom is Within
Bliss is Within

Your heart knows
Sense this remembrance
Soul is always connected
Made from Source

Constant Connection
Divine Presence Creation
Soul speaks to the Heart
You are Divinity

Mystery of Life

Souls search the world
To know their origin
Their true essence
Find the connection

A deep longing
Unanswered questions
Pain and darkness
Loss and regret

The Earth School
Lessons and Homework
Field Trip in physical form
Tests and Major Exams

You came here to be tested
Preparation for the next level
Stay focused, awake, and aware
Sleep no more in class

Graduation is coming
Complete all your lessons
Before your last breath
A Large Banquet Awaits You

Light and Darkness

You are on a quest
In a lower dimension
Where darkness exists
Suffering and tears

You are the Light
From the Greater Light
Shine Your Brilliancy
Dispel the Darkness

Lightworkers came to Earth
Bringing their Light
You are the torch
Service to the Divine Plan

Darkness Disappears
When the Light
Walks into the room
Lightworker Soul

Delight in your Luminosity
Courage with this mission
Graduation from this life
Full understanding of duality

Expression

You needed to experience
Personal Expression
Apparent Separation
Physical Manifestation

Wave after Wave
Life is Expression of you
Who are you really?
An image of Source in Form

Life is a gift, not punishment
When you leave the physical realm
Your viewpoint advanced
A deep knowingness

I am here with you
We are never apart
Your Soul is an aspect
A piece of the Divine Essence

Saturation

Soul and the Divine
Same One Essence
You know all my dreams
Deep connection with you

Unable to sleep
Head spinning
Heart yearning
Love Saturation

Dived into the ocean
Absorption with you
Immersion with Love
Gave in completely

Never want to leave
Enthrallment with you
Obsession with my Beloved
Complete concentration

Treasure our moments together
No one suspects our union
Internally Yours
You know me intimately

My life is yours
You always had my heart
Remembrance of you awakened
Surrendered to Beloved entirely

Happiness

Laughing heartily
Singing loudly
Dancing with music
Heart rejoicing

Movement with Love
Delight at play
Adventure in life
Picnic with friends

Happiness spreads the joy
Bliss in physical realm
Heaven on Earth
Paradise found together

Nirvana in enjoyment
Utopia of cheerfulness
Euphoria Garden
Love is Happiness

Delight of Service

You are the Essence
Permeates everything
You are the sweet perfume
Divine Essence of Love

Humans react from their pain
Put on the Armor of Light
Respond with deep compassion
Earth School is intensive

Surrender your mind, body, personality
To this All-Pervading Divine Presence
It is a gentle breeze
A song of a bird

Life Force within All
This Divine intoxication
Causes this transformation
Oneness with All

Essence of All Essence
Pathway to you is Love
Your sweet aroma
Exposes my true identity

You are the incense
Embraces me gently
My life is not mine anymore
You have me completely

My steps daily are led by you
I am humbled by your Love
This Soul sings in Delight of Service
Gift of Life in the human temple

Song of Oneness

I know you crave connection
Yearning for the Love
I am right here with you

You say you cannot see me
Look deeper and know
I AM within you and All

You enjoy celestial music
Once you can hear
The Song of Oneness

Mystical Experiences
Provide the proof
Deep knowingness

Riddle of Life Revealed
Soul treasures the One Song
All-pervading Divine Symphony

Melody of the Sound Current
Life Force that sustains
Universes upon Universes

Eternity is beyond the reasoning
of the mind, ego, and personality
Song of Oneness constantly playing

Look for those who can teach you
To hear this rapturous music
Song of Oneness playing within

Seek and Find

You came from Love
Will return back
To the Great Love

Wise Ones know
Wonder of Wonder
Manifestation of Light and Sound

Souls incarnate into Earth School
Spend your life wisely
Seek the highest attainment

Life is the opportunity
Preparation for transition
Returning back Home

Seek and Find
Reason for existence
Life lessons and goals

Divine Presence
Always watching
Waiting for your attention

Purification of the mind
Is the journey worth taking
Ultimate discovery of Oneness

Within All

You are the flower
That grows in the garden
You are the cloud
Floating and changing form
You are the laughing child
Running and dancing at play

You are the Celestial Music
Singing in my ears
You are the brilliant sun
Warming and causing growth
You are the forest and plants
Where the wind whispers to them

You are the animals
Communication with each other
You are planets, stars, galaxies
Source Symphony sustains the universe
You are Souls in human form
Disguised yet Wise Ones
See you within All

Service to the Divine Plan

Love of All Loves
Essence within All forms
You sang to me at night
Serenading with your love call
I did not hear you
You kept whispering to me
Distracted by appearances

Wise Ones entered my life
Taught Ancient Spiritual Wisdoms
Now I see you everywhere
Connection with All Life
Attainments completed
Accepted assignment
Divine Melody intoxicating

Spiritual Vortex whirling
Wrapped in your love
Beloved's arrow pierced my heart
Hearing the Sound Current
Transformation of Life
Revelation of True Essence Within
Service to the Divine Plan

Expansion

Your story is a Waking Dream
Each moment through your
Thoughts, emotions, actions
This is a temporary perception

You are infinite and create many stories
Expansion of Consciousness results
You find your place in the Light
Many have misperceptions of Source

Source Light Frequency is Love
Some believe God is angry, controlling
Reference your scriptures to see
Great Spirit is harmony of Love

God of Scripture Texts
Not projected accurately
Magnificent Source is Real, Infinite, Powerful
Love never destroys, only unites

Is Love within your own heart?
In the past, humans did blood sacrifices
Rituals masqueraded as Love
Source never causes war, confusion, hatred

Humans place their emotions onto Source Light
Collective Consciousness of humans creates
Temples of Energy in the Astral plane
You create temples unseen with your thoughts

Astral plane reflects the mind of all Souls
Light and Darkness exist in Astral realm
Connect with the Divine Presence Within
Sacred Love will carry you on your journey

Crystals

Consciousness thrives within Crystals
Power of Light in Crystals
Earth filled with Crystal energy
Set intensions of Love and Service

There is indeed a Sacred Presence
Crystals provide communication assistance
Liquid Crystals are within the human body
Crystals are Friends of Light

Your physical form is a projection
Of your Higher Self to serve you
In this Waking Dream incarnation
Human body vibrating particles of Source Light

Light and Sound frequencies
Picked up by the Crystals in the body
Crystals amplify the signals and store energy
Light within the DNA makes liquid crystals

Pineal Gland Crystal in human brain
Conductor sending and receiving Source Light
All that you seek is within your consciousness
Crystals serve you in revealing Truth

You are a Divine Being
Human brain is a powerful conduit
Communication of Light and Sound frequencies
Crystals are the link between visible and invisible

Expanded Consciousness provides wisdoms
Activation of the Pineal Gland
Divine Connection and unity with life
Crystals serve in assistance to higher levels of consciousness

An Agreement

Great Awakening on Earth
Lightworkers here in service
Holding the Light in place
You volunteered to come here
Purpose work is before you

Explosion of Sound, Color of Light
Grand Shift will cause Bliss
Collective Consciousness will experience One Love
Elohim Souls create with intention, purpose
Awake and Awareness with peace

An Agreement was made between Soul and Source
In one breath, Soul opens the eyes
Life begins in human temple
Your life will have Infinite Light and Power
After assignment, return to Home of Origin

Nothing in your life is wasted
Your profound Love
Will spread to others
When each Soul leaves form
Saturation of Soul in Majestic Love

Frequencies of Light
Magnifications of Color
Glorious Symphony of Sound
Magnificent Harmony of Love
Royal Birthright as a Soul

Soul uses these Truths
Expressing Life in Waking Dreams
You never die in any lifetime
Only leave the Waking Dream
Return to Blissful Peace and Full of Joy

Love Spell

How can I express my Love?
Words fall short in sharing
Deep inner essence inside
You have cast a Love Spell
Caught by your mystical Love
Your sweet melodies in my ear
Unable to focus, Love Currents energize me
Feeling you are near me
Smell of your intoxicating perfume
Divine Essence loving me deeply
Drunk from your Love Spell Wine
My heart is captivated
Constant thoughts of you
The Beloved has me completely
Heaven and Earth have combined
Two energies as One
Spiritual Union of Love
Love Spell whispers to me
My heart aches for more
Inner conversations hearing you saying
I sent you here to know
Difference between Light and Darkness
You are only here for a short stay
Your heart is our connection
This Love is the most glorious
Magnificent Royal Soul
My Darling Brilliant Star
Shine brighter than ever before
How can I love you more?
You are My Essence incarnated

Homesick

How is it that Love endures?
It is a constant power
Only need to tap into it
Feeling far away?
Love is always there
Waiting to be experienced
I know you feel apart
In a distant land
You have not been exiled
Experiencing the physical realm
A foreigner in a foreign land
Homesickness is remembering
Your Home of Origin
Family of Light feels your pain
You visit them at night
Traveling Home for visits
Upon waking, feeling the separation
Deep down knowing never alone
You are here on assignment
Stay the course, earn your medals
Complete your mission
Welcome Home Celebration Banquet
Awaits you on Final Return

Seagull

First day to fly out of the nest
My Seagull parents see my anxiety
They encourage me saying
"It is your time to fly free
You were born to
Soar through the wind
Ride the air currents
Sky Dance with your friends
Enjoy the freedom of flight"
I muster up my courage
Feet perched on the edge of the nest
A high tree I find myself in
Looking down to see a far distance below
Will my wings carry my weight?
Never done this before
Divine Almighty, help me!
I am leaving my home today
A pivotal moment
Moving my feet, flapping my wings
Getting ready for First Flight
Everyone says I am ready
I can do this! I can do this!
Mantra singing in my head
Okay, it is all or nothing
There is no going back
Once I leave this nest
Why did I have to be born a bird?
Animals do not have this challenge
My parents keep saying
"Stop looking Down!
Look to the sky!
Focus! Go airborne!"
This is not to be taken lightly

Do I have to leave the nest today?
All my brothers and sisters are now flying
I am the only one left in the nest
This is the day I have been dreading
My parents are on the branch next to me
Then flying in and out of the tree
Providing inspirational instruction
I am watching them
They are saying my wings are strong
Time has come to trust my abilities
Okay, here I go!
Flapping my wings is lifting my feet up
From the security of the nest
I tuck my feet up against me
Move my head outward thrusting energy
My wings are carrying me forward!
Alleluia! I am flying!
I take to the sky and join other birds
My inner guidance system
Choreographs my flight movements
I let out my Seagull cry with enthusiasm
Wind current moves around my body
Moving my wings to navigate the wind
Soaring came natural with total freedom
My new friends are going to the beach
They are saying it is time to go eat
I see them doing nosedives
Straight into the ocean going for fish
Oh my goodness!
Is that how my parents brought food home?
I just got this flying completed
Now I have to learn nose-diving into the sea
I watch and learn, taking instructions
I fly close to the ocean looking for fish
Seeing an opportunity, upward movement
Then straight down plunging into the sea, I caught the fish!
Today was the beginning, a new life for me

Soaring in the sky is my favorite
Feeling the power of the wind
Air currents carry me to distant islands
I am happy I was born a Seagull
Constant adventures await me

Mother Ayahuasca

Mother of Souls
Goddess of Power
Healing, Protective, Loving
Great Awakener

Mystical Experiences Facilitator
Welcome visits back Home
Sacred Ceremony Initiation
Bonding with human DNA

Soaring with the Light
Gliding through dimensions
Waking up the Lightworkers
Hearing the call to action

Remembering assignments
Piercing the Darkness
Brighter Lights walking the Earth
Community of Strength

Showing the way
My Darling Souls
You are precious Blessed Ones
I Am with you Forever

Always More

Always More Heights
To climb, explore, experience
More love, joy, laughter

Higher-level attainments
Higher-level service
Forever expanding

Advancement of Consciousness
Expansion is your legacy
Adventures through the cosmos

Riding the Infinite Sound Current
You are the reflection
Infinity in physical form

Progression of evolvement
Vastness with Light
Luminary spheres immensity

Magnitude of Life
Love shows way Home
Absolute speaks through poetry

Never an end to expansion
You will spend eternity
Experiencing Always More

Come Back Home

Dear Cherished Soul
Are you really happy in this world?
Could you be searching for something more?
Are you tired of chasing desires?
Feeling that void inside?
Go ahead, dive into the
Ocean of Love and Mercy
Nothing deeper than spending
Eternity with overwhelming Love

Come back Home to the Light
Leave this dark world behind
Stay close to the Divine Essence
Don't believe the darkness
You are Magnificent
A Shining, Brilliant Star
Your radiance causes illumination
Enjoy the Oneness now

Infinite Journey

True happiness comes
From Infinite Presence
Light and Sound, Attributes of Source
Desire to enjoy, Bliss of Oneness
Learning Duality is necessary
Pain and Suffering
Joy and Laughter
Lessons from life experiences
You have always been a Soul
On an Infinite Journey
Vast inner wisdoms
Advances in consciousness
Spiritual path within you
You come to know
Spiritual pathway and you are One
Oneness pervades among Universe
Highest Truth is an inward gaze
You have the right to be happy
Stay with Infinite Presence
Your Soul will take you there
Life Force in all things
Look deeper to all of life
Awareness of Source
Disguised Within
Love the Divine more
Than anything else
Do not get lost in the world
Soul's Journey consists of
Overwhelming lower dimensions of
Physical, emotional, mental levels and
Experience glorious realms of Oneness

Pure Awareness

Highest Truth is
Beyond dimensions of
Relative Truth, Duality
Absolute Truth is
Beyond all dream states of Source

Source is Absolute Truth
Pure Awareness Within
All Seen and Unseen
You are being guided
Journey will bring many options

Choose the highest pathway
You are never limited
Feel the peace and silence
Connect with your Higher Self
You are Love of Source

Can experience this Love
In this present moment
Infinite Presence is
Everywhere and Within All
Soul requires physical life

To experience all potentialities
Soul needs to master duality
Requiring incarnation into physical form
Physical body is the temple of the Soul
You will one day wake up from
Waking Dream called Life

Choice

Free Will offers Souls to choose
Play in the Light or Darkness
You were created with the
Highest Frequency of Love

Souls that choose Light
Perspective of Oneness
Compassion for all creation
Souls that chose Darkness

Desire to deceive, turns to evil
Causing them to move away from Source
Souls' choice to work for Divine Plan
Or have rebelled against Divine Plan of Source

Light always prevails over Darkness
Regardless of appearances in lower regions
Souls harmed physically are covered in Light
Return to their dimension of origin

Shine Your Light
Remember Your True Identity
A piece of Source
You have Free Will, Peace is a Choice

Smile within as you feel loved
All around you that is unseen
Transend this reality
Connecting to higher dimensions within

When you awaken to these other realities
You come to remember
Multidimensional Being filled with
Many dimensions and densities

Challenges

Problems will come
Do everything you can toward resolution
Then release to Higher Self
Ask for best possible outcome
For everyone involved

Surrender your attention
Say, "Thy Will Be Done"
Keep focus on Highest Power
Soul, you can stay talking
With Source all day

Practicing the Presence
Remembering deep connection with Source
Each morning waking up
Remember, you are a Soul
On assignment here on Earth

Mission for Source to Divine Plan
Raising the frequency of the world
Keep awareness, you are not from here
Foreigner in a foreign land
A temporary visitor

Detachment brings freedom
From physical, emotional, mental states
Observation of Real from Unreal
Produces detachment
We are all One

Sound Current

Magnificent Sound Current
Going through your beingness
Resets deep-seated grooves
Transforms set behavioral patterns

Accumulating spiritual wisdoms
Powerful Sound Current of Source
Flows continuously showering Love
Healing, gratitude, renewal

Being a unique expression
Peace that surpasses conscious mind
After Mystical Experience
Spiritual student knows

Transformation is now a reality
Dining with Truth provides fruits
Easily revealing spiritual wisdoms
True Essence of arcane mysteries

All are extensions of Divine Absolute
Experiencing creation, Divinity of Source
Manifesting in unique expressions
Duality, catalyst for evolution

Remember your Divine Origin
You are in Cosmic University
Profound connection with Source
Soul saturated with Divine Love

Waking Dream

Realization of this Waking Dream
Removes the power over it
If you get lost in the dream
Reawaken and remember
You are living out experiences
In a lower reality
It is just a dream
Not the highest reality of Source
Your first mistake
Was taking it to be real
Soul awareness awaken
Balance in both worlds
Visible and Invisible
Spiritual life leads the physical life
Illusions of this world
Cause covering over third eye
Awakened consciousness opens
Mysteries of Spirit
Seeker, surrender completely
To Most Powerful Force of Existence
Trust the Living Essence
Created all of life
Contemplate, you are greatly loved
Rely on Infinite Presence Within
Remembering causes wonderful serenity
Flawless vision enters immediately
Ascension of consciousness
Advances viewpoint, transformation
Luminousness transparency
Insights and enthusiasm
Service to the Divine Plan

Spiritual Battle

Light and Darkness
Battle in the lower realms
All-consuming warfare
Humans caught in the middle

Absolute Light always prevails
Remember, you are in the lower kingdom
Where Darkness conquers
Darkness will try to deceive you

Light Warrior, stand in your glory
You cannot achieve your medals
Until you have gone into battle
Lower dimensions are the battlefield

You came here to Shine Powerful Light
Be proud of your battle scars
All Master Soul Teachers
Share about this Spiritual Battle

Between Light and Darkness
You are in a dark world
This is why you came here
Warmth and renewal from Absolute Fire

Darkness will try to overpower you
Connect to your True Identity
Light Warrior, pull out your sword
Put on the Armour of Light

Shine Brightly in a dark world
After completion of Earthly assignment
Upon arrival back Home
Celebration Banquet in your honor

Your friends on the other side of life
Cheer you on, proud of you
Stand tall with courage
Revered precious Light Warrior

Surrendered

You spin my head
Make me dizzy
With your marvelous Love

Unable to think of anything else
You have my Soul
Unable to escape

You have taken me over
I have Surrendered
Cannot resist anymore

My life is yours now
I guess it always has been
Just came to terms with it

Your Divine Essence
Overwhelmingly intoxicating
Life without you is meaningless

My heart was consumed by this world
You came to me and pierced my heart
I will serve you always

Some say it is a burden
I say it is a blessing
Your arrow in my heart

Direct hit in the heart center
Too deep to remove
Union with Beloved's Arrow

Plateau

On a mystical journey
May experience a Plateau
Reaching a higher-vibrational level
You look around seeing no support
Others mastering initial stages

Desiring spiritual mastership
Looking for higher-level community
Master Soul Teacher needed
Mastered these levels, shows by example
Guidance, instruction, spiritual discussions

Mastering of the wisdoms, integration
Evolutionary growth, spiritual mastership
Resource for spiritual student
Remembrance of your True Identity
First step on mystical journey

Beyond duality of love and hate
All is seen clearly, nothing is hidden
Identified with other than Divinity
Seeing everything as separate
Not seeing the Oneness

Try to balance Divinity with human life
A master-level teacher produces
A spiritual master
Master teachers know their time is temporary
Create replacements to teach ready Souls

Seekers send a request to Divine Essence
Loving petition for higher spiritual level
Heartfelt call that goes out
Universe responds lovingly
To any Soul who wants to reunite with Source

A Cry for Meaning

Pain and suffering
Illusion of separateness
Sense of unity comes from the Truth

We are all a part of the One Infinite Essence
Permeates All and IS ALL
Visualizing despair in our culture

Humanity is ready for mystical journey
Sadness, greed, fear, unhappiness
Opportunities for moving to next level

Willingness to search for meaning in life
A situation can cause a person
To look at their life asking for meaning

An Awakened Soul can separate Truth from illusion

Sacrifice

This life is your Sacrifice

Humanity cried out for help
Inspire Brother and Sister Souls

You answered the call
Accepted assignment on Earth
It was harder than expected

The Darkness devours many Souls
Heart of Courage essential
Take up your Sword of Light

Sacrifice sometimes involves
Walking the Path of Light alone

Misunderstood, ridiculed, persecuted
Do not get lost in this dark world
Remember who you are

Magnificent Beautiful Lightworker
You came here to Shine Your Light

You are the comet in the night sky
Blazing radiant speed of brilliancy
While stargazers applaud you

Oneness with Source

Absolute Powerful Source
Knew Itself before creation
Infinite Frequency created out of nothingness
Ethers are filled with Glorious Awareness
Primordial Sound explodes the void of timelessness

Causes the Light to manifest
A wave expanded generating outbursts
Expressions of Itself producing heat and power
Creating suns, pieces would become stars
Expansion bringing forth multiverses

Source Love Frequency
Desired to experience Itself throughout infinity
Many Souls were created
Boundless manifestation of Divine Source
In the beginning First Souls created

Knew themselves as ONE
Other Souls created later would refer to them
As the Elohim, Divine Essence of Source
Only identify themselves with foreverness
Having the power of the ONE

Soul group called Elohim later created bodies
Caused them to know Light and Darkness
All Souls will undergo life in lower dimensions
To comprehend their own creative power
True Divine nature, unique expressivity
Oneness with Source

Divinity

Unfoldment process allows Soul to emerge
Starting the prominent role instead of Ego
At a certain evolutionary level
Discipline is not required

Resistance is absent
Identification with Source is present
An advanced Soul loves all
Realization that Source is Within All

Who are you really?
Source disguised as a human
Your true nature is Divinity
Source lives within you

Divine holds you as a delicate flower
Safeguarding your daily unfoldment
Your greatest lover is within you
All you have to do is turn inward

Accept eternal love of Beloved Source
Oneness of Divinity
We are all ONE family of Divine Beings
We are the collective of the Divine

Profound Soul

Once a Soul has been touched by the Divine
Desiring to become absorbed in the melodies
Harmonic Celestial Symphony
Causes intense intoxication of pure love

Once a certain vibrational level is reached
Higher Self will reveal Itself
To the conscious mind letting be known
Soul now on the ascendent

Soul will calm the mind causing
Surrendering process to begin
Ego becomes intoxicated with Divine melodies
Soul moves toward service to Divine Plan

Dear Profound Soul
You have a unique wavelength
Your spiritual fingerprint
This is your Energetic Signature Frequency

Mind becomes scattered handling daily duties
Bring Soul's energy inward
Communion with the Divine
Allow Soul to remember
Oneness with Pure Source Frequency

Promises of Light

You are Light
You are Power
You are Wisdom
Reach for the Promises of Light
When others attack you with words

Remember, you are infinite
Love cannot be divided or denied
Love is eternal, rest in this love
There is no conflict when you reside in the Light
Find a place that provides peace and live there

You may have to sacrifice familiarity
Peace is priceless
Reside in the highest frequency of Love
You will energetically draw people to you
For the best interest of all

Trust in the Sacred Essence
You carry this power Within
Many Souls need the Light that you carry
You are needed on this planet
Shine brightly in this dark world

Who is the one looking out of your eyes?
You are in this reality with help and assistance
You have friends in high places
Source Frequency is always instantly available
You are a piece of Omnipotent Source

You are a part of everything
Only in this Waking Dream do you feel alone
You are One with Divine Source
A glorious celebration when you return Home
Completion of life story, you have full perception

Story of You

Source emanates from you
You carry this power inside in every moment
Highest perspective is to know you are this Light
Overcome this Darkness that you see around you
Your journey will have peaks and valleys

If a road ends, new beginning awaits you
Darkness may appear to be hindering the Light
The path is the journey to experience Darkness
You are the Light that takes away Darkness
Persevere and conquer all Darkness with your Light

Make decisions benefiting your Soul Life
You are on a Divine Assignment
You are here by design and filled with splendor
Divine Presence experiences all your joys and struggles
Your journey is the Story of You

Light Dispels All Darkness

Primordial Light

Primordial Light becomes human eggs
Ovum egg is a perfect sphere
Egg of Life, sacred geometric pattern
Creates all the living life forms
Light forms bodies, right down to eye color
Primordial Light created you
Light and Sound create geometric patterns
Expand to be called Fruit of Life
Atoms, shape of a sphere
Light waves are spheres moving through space
Atoms create molecules
The fabric of reality
Geometry within human body
Organic chemistry
Atoms sing with Celestial Harmonic Symphony
Light and Sound create all matter in physical reality
You came down here to show how to live
Become an example of a highly evolved being
Show how to live in this low-vibrational reality
Permanent Awareness causes
To live from the Soul State
After tasting the Divine ambrosia
Leaves an imprint for eternity
You are on an inner path
Somewhere along the way
Journey goes inward
Causing direct mystical experience
Changes your viewpoint forever
Desire for higher life
Leads to spiritual liberation
Ever-expanding consciousness
Let your life be a walking Divine reflection

Higher Self and Lower Self

There are two of you
Lower Self: Ego, Mind, Personality
Higher Self: Soul, the I AM, Spark of Source
Transformation is going from one identity to the other
Identification from Lower Self to Higher Self

True identity is the Soul
The adventure, whole spiritual unfoldment
Know the eternal aspect of your own beingness
Live on the energy that inspires us
Along the spiritual journey will experience

Cups of elixir felt as Love Waves
You start to realize there are two of you
Spiritual Life and Temporal Life
You begin to realize who you Really Are
Your identity shifts knowing True Self

Pathway of unfoldment shows Dual Consciousness
Realization, Divine Being feeling love and bliss
Omnipotent Beloved loves you
Spiritual downloads come receiving wisdoms
Stay close to the Beloved

Don't wander off too far …

Love along the Journey

Soul State causes connection toward Divine Presence
Soul and Divine reside within same area
Transformation of Body Consciousness to the Beloved
Natural resonation with Divine Essence

You are connected, forever One
Rising in spirituality shows Ego's antics
Seeing Lower Self, insights
In Soul State, Divine always with you

You can contact that Love any time
View life from Higher Self perspective
You are Divine Being having human journey
In your Soul-ness then Divine flows

Stay in the Soul State of Being
This will naturally occur on the path
Love grows daily for Divine Presence within
Stay in connection, it will happen

No matter what happens in your life
Physical world is just a virtual classroom
When in Higher Self, you are in harmony with the Divine
You have the power, you are the Soul

Upgrade the image of yourself
See yourself as a Divine Being
Take time alone with Divine Presence
Feel this Love along the Journey

Highway of Love

Intense longing and separation, the reaction
Being down here away from Home
Aspect of Divine Presence within you
Those are pains of separation
Remember, you are a Soul, Divine Presence
Separate from your Lower Self, Ego
Easier for Soul State connection

If you find people leaving your life
You no longer have to play out those situations
Received a higher grade on your lessons and tests
When your vibration has been raised
If the other person's frequency is lower
They will leave your life at some point
Sometimes we have to release them for self-preservation

Path never ends
You never end
Will spend eternity in expansion
You never completely arrive
We all will spend eternity expanding, serving Divine Plan
You don't want it to end
Adventures are endless

Love transforms you by your own spiritual beauty
Love purifies the Lower Self
Nothing is superior to Love
Get on the Highway of Love
Eat it, drink it, bathe in it
Love and peace come
With connection to Divine Presence

Poetry is a Song

Consciousness has no form
It deals with Awareness, Truth, Soul
Beyond the Lower Self and is always free
Consciousness is really who you are
Spiritual journey is easy
Mind thinks it is rough

You need to have Love so big
You forget the mind
Your mind is always chirping
Learn to ignore it
Poetry is a song
It has musical vibrations

When you work from the heart, it shows
People will be attracted to it
Going within is what connects you to Source
Be still with Divine Presence
People move to places on Earth
A vibrational match

Be with Souls you resonate with vibrationally
You will thrive
Don't be afraid of shining your light
Master Souls have come to Earth
Even though they were advised
Would be tough assignment

Continuation of Master-Level service
Passing tests in assignment
Toward highest octave, Home Vibration
Humanity is being asked
Hold to higher levels of consciousness
Divine Presence guides you

Enlightenment

When you are enlightened
Sometimes you have to live outside of the tribe
Because you are so different
You are shunned, so you live alone
People come to you for help
One day you won't be seen as odd or strange
You will be seen as balanced

Meaningful life is possible
Find an opportunity to work
In a place that has meaning
Have to come down
To lower physical realm and check on
Younger Souls who are in
Lower grades in the Earth School
We all have to pull rotation in the lower worlds
There is no judgment
It is only an observation

Remember your True Identity
You are a piece of Source in physical form
Having a human experience
You are Source wearing a human disguise
Can be hard to accept since you created
Very powerful Ego to resist this Truth
Love and accept all aspects of your consciousness

Cosmic Drama

You have two choices
Get lost and stay in the story
Or realize you are in a Cosmic Drama
Now create something wonderful
Do not burden yourself with having to
Figure all this out

You can have fun here daily
Walking with your Higher Self
Come to your Divine Essence
Everything can be solved
Coming to Source asking for wisdom
The enemy is only an aspect of your mind

Likes to create drama and villains
Heal this aspect of your mind
Send love and light to this person
Then stay with the Higher Self
Be a peaceful person
Be at peace in your consciousness

Once you move beyond duality
You can experience the Oneness
See the Beloved everywhere
Separation is an illusion
You are in the Waking Dream
Stay awake and aware of it
Mind is into the Cosmic Drama
Soul is in the Oneness of Source

Incarnation

In the beginning of your awakening
You realize you are in captivity
There is another reality
Soul had to take on an incarnation
Experience separation and feel lost
Then awaken to realize
This life was to gain experience
In the physical realm
You step into this life
Get lost in the Waking Dream
Then get awakened to see

You are in a dilemma
A world of illusions, a temporary life
You are a Divine Being
Having a physical life
The goal is realizing
When Ego is in control
You can move into the Soul State
Stay in the Higher Self perspective
Do not get lost in this incarnation
Your curriculum is for you to awaken
From the illusion of separation from Source

Dark Night of the Soul

Dark Night of the Soul is when
You realize that in order to stay awake
You have to step away from all those
Inducements that cause you
To get lost in the Waking Dream

You are heartbroken because you feel
You won't get to experience all the
Excitement that caused you
To dive into this intense life

The pain is realizing, just a playground
You see all these Souls running around
Playing in the playground
Lost in this holographic reality

The mind makes you believe it's real
You realize that intensity is gone
That came from being lost
In the drama of life

Earth School allows the Soul to
Explore this play and then awaken
Out of the illusion of separateness
Practice spending time beyond this drama

Be okay with leaving form and going back Home
We just drop the garment of the body
It is safe, natural, freeing
We are Source Energy Beings Individualized

Empowerment

Trust, Relax, Know
No matter what happens
It will benefit you
Could take years to finally see this

Rest in this wisdom
No matter what happens
No matter how things look
It will always benefit you

This is the position of power
This is Self-Empowerment
Stay with this viewpoint
Unless you like to suffer

Separation is an illusion
How can one be separated when made of Source?
Soul is a piece of Omnipotent Source Essence
We are Source Individualized having a human experience

Ego/Mind is the filter between Soul and Source
Soul will say, "Pain is separation from Divine."
We get lost in the Ego
Feeling this separation

You have worth
You are precious
You are Loved
You are a Divine Being

Spiritual Master in training
Proud of your courage, strength, perseverance
Forgive so you can move on
Move forward with your life

Real Love

Anger is when you don't feel loved
Many people are missing love
Use compassion toward other people
They could be going through difficulties
Remember this is your mission

This is developing your skills
There are hostile people here on Earth
They don't know Real Love here
Goal is to be more loving
Lightworkers are living in two worlds

World of Matter and World of Eternity
This is what we do here on planet Earth
You don't diminish when you share infinitely
We are representatives of Source Light
Your consciousness needs to be high enough

To love and care about people
Don't be triggered by their Ego and pain
Move beyond survival and thrive
Everyone is applauding you
Understand the mission

Brought Light into Darkness

In the beginning there was Infinite Darkness
You brought Light into this Dark World
How can you fix or clean it without experiencing it?
If you are not bringing Light to it
You end up with victimhood
Only a messed-up person would abuse another person

Ego gets hurt, not the Soul
Sometimes your Higher Self will create the storm
In order for you to turn within
Difficult people were abused themselves
See them as Source sees them
You can be the Light to your friends

Say to the Divine Presence
"Thy Will Be Done"
Surrender your life to the Divine Plan
Find people who match your frequency
Be a living example
Living a healthy life

Learn how to practice nonreaction
We have lots of feelings
Let things happen and unfold for you
Find joy in everything you do
You are turning on, being activated, remembering
You are shifting into a higher frequency

Evolved

Soul creates diverse realities
To see different aspects of itself
You have created every perspective
We are projecting this reality
Love all the projections of yourself
Vibration of Sound is the energy of Light
Source creates the Soul
Soul creates the physical form
Ascension from every experience
Evolution primary cause for being
Wisdom for understanding of Truth
Divine cares if you have learned
Evolved from your experiences
Universe provides process of elevation
Intensity of Light will increase on this planet
At same time the intensity of Darkness
You are here to hold your ground
Stand in the Darkness
You never run from Darkness
Stand in it and hold your position
Being in this low frequency is painful
Some days it can be agony
Remember you are in a matrix
See through this physical illusion
Appears real while you experience it
Light you hold is more powerful than Darkness
Darkness cannot diminish Your Light
This is why you are on this planet
You are the Lighthouse, Lightworker, Light Warrior
Showing the way to the Light
Stand in the chaos, empowered Divine Light Being
You are an expression of the Divine Essence

Light Warrior

Set realistic expectation about perfection
Being in an Enlightened State of Being
Does not mean nothing bothers you

You are in human form
Will experience emotions impacting you
You are here to feel and experience

Will feel the pain, suffering, evil, corruption
Have absolute perception of who you are inside
World of illusion in physicality

Master this illusion by staying awake
True identity of Divine Being in physical form
You are the Warrior of Light

Lift your glorious formidable sword
Pierce the Darkness
You came here to shine

World of the Ego

World of the Ego is Duality
Spiritual student wants to move into
Dimensions above the Ego
Soul gets caught in illusion of Waking Dream
After leaving realm of Source
Travels downward into Dream World
Adventures for Self-Discovery
Journey of the Soul
One day Soul wakes up
Remembers Soul's True Identity
In captivity of the Ego
Goal to leave dimensions of duality
Soul wants to travel Home
Absorption and union with Source
Your unique individual awareness is not lost
Divine Being, Spiritual Royalty, Soul
Ego whispers lies into your ears
Ego wants to keep control over the Soul
Once awakened to True Identity as Divine Being
Soul steps into first position
Ego steps back and serves Soul's wishes
In beginning of journey Ego will fight the Soul
Celestial Sound soothes, spiritualizes Ego
Ego gives up the fight
Forever serves the Soul
Soul loves service to Divine Plan
Ego detains Soul in lower world
Ego needs the energy of the Soul
To survive and stay in control
Stay awake and aware of Ego's tricks
Keeping you in bondage to the lower realms
Staying awake in Waking Dream is your power

Transcendence

Evolutionary Transcendence of Unity
Higher-level of awareness knows you need to transform
Your reality into another one of higher frequency
Ego says, "I don't want to change"

Hence your reality is changed by force
Primary expression of the universe is ascendence
You shift through surrender or force
Be in the flow of harmony

Evolving the viewpoint of your life
Live in harmony in all aspects of your life
Spiritual law of acceptance
Offers seeker to accept more changes

As you move higher, will be willing to change
Changes may appear not good
Keep moving onward and upward to higher ground
Challenges are part of the climb

Your Higher Self will lead you
Problems are opportunities, what Soul requires
Right view, right thought, right action, purification process
Soul says, "Keep moving upward"

Move, move, move, stay going forward
Your assignment is causing you to keep going
Your life itself is the journey
Transcendence sees all situations from Soul perspective

Between Life and Death

Individuality of the Soul wanted to go out
Have direct experience of life
You can be homeschooled for only so long
Need to go off to Cosmic University
Soul leaves Source and comes to Earth
Soul has lessons and exams in Earth School
All paths lead to Source
Promote love on Earth
Wisdom taught by Master Souls
What really counts is what you did
Between Life and Death on this planet
Love is the name used for resonance
Resonate to level of love
Integrates with Divine Presence
Must become what you want
Harmonizing becoming One
Remember is to Re-Member with all that is
It is Love, for consciousness loved Itself
Had no others to resonate with
Oneness is discovered
Spiritual practice offers ecstasy with Divine Love
Allows time away from the Ego
Connection to Divine Presence seen everywhere
Lovers listen to Higher Self
Remain in communication with Divine Essence
Divine Source says
"I want you for myself, don't want to share you with the Ego"

True Essence

May all living beings prosper, have peace, good fellowship
Send out good wishes for the highest
Wishing best welfare of entire universe

When Soul connects with Source
Receives infinite power of strength
While in a body here is immense power within

This power is Omnipotent Source
Soul and Source are One
This is the highest Truth

Existence of Source is invisible
Divine Essence cannot be seen by physical eyes
Source dwells within, illuminates our Soul

If you need help, ask your Higher Self
Know that Divine is with you
Infinite Presence is your True Essence

Deep Connection

Darkness exposed by Power of Truth
Darkness based on falsehood, deception
Light of Truth exposes lies, corruption
Showing the weak side of Darkness
Vast establishments afraid of losing power
Caused by humanity awakening from ignorance

Spiritual Master Souls who have walked this planet
Awareness revealed by highest truths
Teach Souls spiritual mastery, attainments
How to stay in higher states of being
Living above the ego, personality, shadow

High level of mastery
Causes nonduality consciousness level
Comes a stage on spiritual path
Feelings are expressed from heart
A real yearning comes within yourself
Kindles the fire that burns away attachments
To the ego and outer world

Lovers for the Beloved
Produce this yearning of deep connection
A memorable event creates this yearning
To return to this indescribable state

Light of Truth

Spiritual inspiration fuels one's life
Desires fade away compared to highest realized state
State of the Lover for the Beloved
Dedicates their life into service toward Divine Plan
Uncomfortable to the Seeker

Until mystical experience occurs
Deep inner awareness of true identity
As Source manifested to experience Itself
If someone deeply injures you
Allow them to stay in their darkness

You cannot fix or change their behavior
Surrender the situation to Divine Essence
Move onward knowing at some point
This person will experience what you went through
On the other side of the veil during Life Review process

After leaving this life
Every person goes through Life Review
Viewing how their life affected others
All is revealed in the Light of Truth
Nothing is hidden from All-Pervading Eye

Sleep no more dear Soul
Your Soul has been pierced by the arrow
Beloved is waking you up from this dream

Fathom the Splendor

Source resides forever in your Soul
Entire ocean can't drown it
Forest fire can't burn it
No one can take this from you
Your Soul has been pierced by the arrow
Awake from this ocean of existence

Come beyond pain and agony
Find the narrow path, reach the far shore
Never look at this temporary world the same way again
Give meaning to your life
Connect with your infinite Divinity
Supreme Source will fill your Soul with joy

Only the Soul can Fathom the Splendor
Of this state of being
Ego makes us feel this outer reality is real
Outer world like an amusement park
A wise Soul chooses to go inward
Connect to real joy Divine offers them

Your Ship Has Come In

Source music, primordial sound
Unstruck symphony, eternal power of creation
Countless Souls are awakened
Hearing Celestial harmonic frequencies
Beloved is beyond names, forms, origin of everything
Before creation, continues throughout eternity
Beloved leaves home, takes on form
Gathers the Souls who are ready
Reminds them of long-forgotten realm
Your ship has come in, don't delay
Step on board to become awakened
Free yourself from rituals, fear, this dream
For many Souls it has become a nightmare
Supreme Source's Voice is the Sound Current
Is calling you home to remember your origin
You have played in the playground of existence
Now being called back Home
You are Divine Beings, remember your Divinity
Retrace your journey toward original home
You are very close
You don't have far to travel
Only the veil between you and home
Is the world of the Ego

Ego's Web

We are caught in the agony of Ego's Web
Escape is to drop the sense of separate existence
What is the goal? Ultimate Awareness
Source within pervades all and Is All
Source offers Free Will
Ignore or accept loving offer
To connect with eternal spring of Divine Love
Always room available at banquet table
You can drink the poison of this temporary world
Or partake in ambrosia of Divine treasure
Awakened Souls are connected to Divine Presence
Connect your hearts to the Beloved
End the agony of Ego's Web
Pain of separation is so intense, anguishes constantly
We fill it with temporary delights
Nothing fills this starvation
Realms of existence are nothing to us
A knife stabbing at our hearts
Nothing compares to the ceaseless celestial melody
Absorption, love, reverence
Allows us to lose our connection with temporary world
We have been asked to serve humanity
Help them remember their Divinity

Know Thyself As Divinity

Unfoldment comes in each moment
You have within you resources
Can handle every experience
Your Soul is very powerful
You chose to yield to circumstances
Knowing the Waking Dream being temporary
Your True Essence, your True Self
Can never be harmed
You are dealing with situations
In far reaches of Eternity
We experience pain and joy
You chose to step away from Infinite Bliss
To experience the human journey
This Waking Dream for many became a nightmare
Know your True Identity
Piece of Source, a Soul, in human form
Offers you the opportunity to feel your power
Continue to move beyond
Connect with Higher Self
Your Light is so vast
You walk through Darkness
Exposes your Divinity, Power, Authority
When you step to the other side of life
You will know you are a Divine Being
Your brilliant Light is stunning!
Waking Dream is duality, is temporary
Know Thyself As Divinity
You are the sacred Essence of Source

Vastness inside of You

You can't even imagine the vastness inside of you
Huge regions are waiting for you to explore
Keep going so you can see them
Stay moving forward in your self-discovery
Awakening to your Divinity is only the beginning
Experiencing a holographic reality, Waking Dream
You perceive this reality as real, only One
There are many realities
Your ego covers your True Identity
Wise Souls want to see their powerful Divinity
You have Free Will
Choose Light, conquer Darkness
Go within to this place of peace
You are the collective Divinity
The One Divine Source
To know of our Divinity and union with Source
Greater than all collected wealth in the world

Abundance of Jubilation

You can go through life searching
Celestial music filled with bliss
This Divine Melody is within you
Tap into this Abundance of Jubilation
Take time often to free your heart
Feel this Divine Love, you carry it within
There is no shortage, available to everyone

Go to a memory when you experienced enjoyment
It is free to delight in
More joy you give away, more it grows
Everyone is hungry for happiness
Even animals enjoy being happy

Why does sadness exist?
How else would you know true treasure of joy?
You need to experience all emotional states
A single memory can turn your life around
A frequency is assigned to each emotion
Take a cup and dip into your reservoir of blissful love

Magnificent Journey

You are on a magnificent journey of self-discovery
Launched into a reality of the unknown
Learning valuable lessons in the Earth School
Overcoming challenges, experience corruption
Awaken to the wisdom where transformation occurs
Rebirth set you onward toward your return home
You have your own unique journey
Continue moving forward, pathway may feel too steep
You may feel you are on the side of a mountain
A small step is movement forward
Journey is about you
You are Divine Royalty
Upon return home, transformation, deeper understanding
Remembering your true identity transforms your consciousness
All that you need is within you
God Realization is not that far off
It is right within you
Saying to the child that adulthood is within them
Stay connected to Divine Presence
When someone is mean and hurtful
Know that their Ego is torturing them
Try not to react and stay calm
Only the Ego is sensitive and reacting
Goal of spiritual path of love
Become one with Self and Source
Ego is standing in the way
When on a spiritual journey of love
Develop your inner life with Divine Presence
Who is with you at all time
We can get lost in this outer life
Deep spiritual journey is balance between inner life and outer life

Spiritual Phone to Call Home

Widespread loneliness on this Earth
Identity with Ego, false sense of identity
Results in feeling separate and alone
While in physical form in world of Ego
Feeling of separateness caused by illusion of Ego
Barrier between Soul and Source
Soul cannot be separate from what it's made of
Soul has constant union with Divine Essence
Pains of separation from Source are very real
Intensity felt many times daily
Develop spiritual practice to connect
Time in union with Source helps
You visit home for a while
It is bittersweet, you are happy, feel deeply loved
You know you will have to step back to Earth life
Need to play in separation for further evolution
You can go visit home at any time
Helps in staying awake in the Waking Dream
Gone off to a distant school away from home
Many Souls feel homesick
When feeling alone, go within, connect
Can go outside the Ego identity
You are a Soul, your true identity
While at distant school can call home
Connection through different spiritual practices
You are unique, any connection is all that matters
Divine Presence is within you
Can call home at any time
To connect, feel loved, encouragement to keep going
Pick up the spiritual phone to call home
When you feel alone or overwhelmed
Spiritual community helps with outside connection
Hugs from friends do wonders for homesickness

Spell of Illusion

Souls in conflict under spell of illusion
They won't understand evolved awakened Souls
Look at people as Souls, not mere humans
Most people caught up in illusion of separateness

Awakened Souls see the Oneness of Source
Within themselves and within all
Further travel along spiritual pathway
More observer of life

Your journey moves you to Absolute Oneness
Love and Oneness
Separateness and loneliness
Evil is based on extreme separateness

Each Soul chooses to move closer to the Light of Source
Or away through ill-thought-out causes
Free Will toward Darkness of Separation
Absolute reality is Source and Oneness

We have Free Will to choose in realms of duality
Each Soul comes into illusion to learn
Divine Presence within All and IS ALL
When illusion removed, only Source exists

Higher Viewpoint

Unawakened Souls unaware of effects on others
Forgive them for their ignorance
Many Earth's residents in initial stage of reawakening
They don't understand their patterns are destructive

Only awakened Souls know path of peace, love, balance
Walk Divine inspirational life
Along spiritual pathway, personal Ego gets put aside
Replaced with Soul leading life

Brings acceptance of human journey
Major exams in Earth School extremely overwhelming
Handle them with fortitude and strength
Keep moving forward even with small steps

You eventually get to top of mountain
Much higher viewpoint changes your perspective
Viewpoint on top of mountain much superior
To the one held while standing at ground level

Aware Souls focus their life
Service to the Divine Plan
Releasing personal will for Divine Will

Light Armor

You are a powerful Divine Being
Came with fruitful gifts
Everything is here for your realization
Earth School allows becoming familiar
What is real and what is illusion

What is lasting and what is temporary
Connection to Divine Awareness is real
Connection to Infinite Love is real
Spirit, consciousness, Power of Light is real
Energy living in all Souls is real

You have a protective Light around
Infinite Energy of creation is beating your heart
Every morning put on your Light Armor
See your Light Shield in place
Your Soul is the frequency of Source

Infinite Spirit is your essence
Awareness of your Divine nature
You are meant to bloom with serenity

Collective Neurosis

What is up is down and what is down is up
Collective neurosis is dysfunctional society
Trends and delusions considered the skill
To function within a dysfunctional collective
Many Egos together create an Ego society

People become functional in collective neurosis thinking
Ego identity causes conflict and division
Enlightened Ones who step out of society
Remove themselves as much as possible
They recognize the dysfunction

Greed, judgment, jealousy, betrayal, hatred
Dysfunctional forms of mental illness
Many Souls move to a community for Divine Consciousness expression
Enlightened Souls know themselves to be unique expressions of Source
Wise Souls do not serve rules that don't benefit life on this planet

Enlightened Souls viewed as unusual, odd, misunderstood
Advanced society, no court needed, no police, no religion
Filled with Master-Level spiritual Souls
Recognize they are a piece of Source, serve Divine Will

Evolved Souls see this life as an opportunity of service
Divine Plan, Soul growth, true-identity of Oneness with Source

Quest for Meaning

Quest for meaning begins, seeking mysteries of life
Why am I here?
Where did I come from?
Am I being tested?
What happens when I die?

Did I have goals to accomplish in this life?
Many questions arise
Quest for Meaning begins expedition
At end of journey will remember this illusion of Waking Dream
Only Source exists, recognition of true identity

You are a piece of Source in human form
You are a Divine Being
Source creates to express through creations
We are all Source's expressions
Your life is Source's creation and love for you

Truth sets us free from personal Ego identity
Soul remembers its Oneness with Source
True spiritual teachers will teach students of their own divinity
Higher-level Souls serve the Divine Will
Knew mission prior to incarnation into physical form

While on Earth have Awakening of assignment
No personal choice since they are in Oneness with Divine Will
Source makes the choice
Higher Light Hierarchs from Cosmic University
Teach and awaken ready Souls for total awakening

A Master Soul helps them understand deeper wisdoms
Cosmic Consciousness, Nonduality, Self-Realization
God Realization, Spiritual Evolution

Higher States of Being

Utmost spiritual experience occurs within the Seeker
Teacher guides, mentors, explains
Student can connect, listen to inner guidance
Direct mystical experience is ultimate teacher within you

High-level teachers raise consciousness of those on Earth
Ready to go into higher states of being
Source within the spiritual teacher
Attracts Souls ready to remember

Source provides the instruction
Spirit Guides of each Soul will guide them
To the highest-vibrational spiritual teacher
Receiving highest frequency, raising student's love

See and know that All is Source
Manifesting in many different forms
Once Source has individualized as a Soul
Only appears separated from Oneness with the Divine

Source cannot create anything separate from Itself
Only appearance of separateness

Divine Shines through You

When a person experiences the Ego death
False sense of identity of personal Ego temporarily removed
Soul experiences Oneness
Connection with Supreme Source

Ego is the barrier to Oneness with Divine Love
Lower personal Ego, more Divine Presence
Know your true identity
Unique expression of Absolute Source

Accept this temporary physical life is Waking Dream
We are Divine's Will individualized
One of the goals is to be a reflection
Divine Presence within covered by flesh

Let the Divine Shine through You
Allow your luminescence to reflect the Beloved
Always with you and is you
Higher ultimate reality is possible

After Awakening occurs
Personal will influenced by Divine Will
At higher state of being
Days filled with service to Divine Plan

Ego no longer in charge, running your life
Awakened person guided by Divine Presence
Thy Will Be Done
New motto and expression

Descent into Darkness

Time to experience Darkness
Descended from your home of origin
All the way down through the dimensions
Numerous characteristics clung to you
These qualities needed for Earth life
Oscillation frequencies changed as you descended
Increasingly darker and darker
Energy became denser
Your body appeared and covered your Soul
Destiny set, goals, lessons, mission
Birthed into this life, now on Earth
Learned local culture, language atmosphere
Assignment started, new life begun
Awakening occurs, spiritual battlefield
Warned would be difficult, filled with traps
Adversary's kingdom flooded with Darkness
Your sword well used to fight dark angels
Luminosity of your Soul, Beacon of Powerful Light
Shining radiantly reduces the Darkness
Awakens other Souls sleeping
Your purpose work in action
Reason for being on Earth
Darkness will whisper lies to you
Light always wins
Darkness disappears immediately when light arrives
Your illumination is essential
Brave beautiful Soul, shine brilliantly
Stand victoriously against the Darkness

Origins Unveiled

Magnificent Souls, you have incarnated
To an adversarial planet
Helping to raise consciousness level
Human collective asleep to true identity

Do your best to live in this Waking Dream
Live in a way that allows you to follow your heart
Do what brings you joy
Connect with others whom you resonate with

Supportive of your spiritual journey
You walk and live among a species unaware
Humans are Divine Beings, spiritual royalty
Origin of Oneness with Source

You are with Divine Presence
The Beloved at all times
Some days you will yearn for your home of origin
Physical life is a temporary exploration in illusion

Cannot be separate from what you are made of
Glorious Divine Being, a piece of Source
You are the wave, Source is the ocean
You are the plant, Divine is the soil

You are the bird, Cosmic Supreme is the sky
You are the instrument, Divine Symphony is the music
You are the radiant star, Celestial Essence is the universe
You are a Divine Being, Infinite Presence in human temple

Rebirth of the Soul

Love is shortcut to Divine Essence
Divine Love is eternal
Other types of love perish with time
Craving this permanent love
Personify a higher state of being
Spiritual exercises, purification of the Ego
Soul loses interest in dazzle of the world
Senses pull away seeing emptiness, temporary, illusion
Now the Soul is free from bondage of senses
Captivity caused separation
Soul can now immerse itself
Oneness in spiritual union
Divine Essence places you on a quest
Union with the Beloved
Your union was never broken
Ego was the only obstacle
Arrive to awareness
View your pure dazzling essence
When Source rules your heart
Profound connection
Experiencing land of the Ego
You are in a temporary school
Ego tries to trick us
Make us believe away and separate from Source
Once Soul awakens to learn of Divinity
Quickly soars home
Reacquaints with true identity
A piece of Source
Soul is eternal, immortal, pure energetic luminosity
Master Souls teach of this separate ego
Our life can be lived through Ego or Divine Love
Once Soul is freed from Ego, loses fear and bondage
Soul lives in freedom, Ego lives in fear

Rise

Mind labels everything good and bad
Soul views everything as an experience
Evolution of consciousness allows to see
Beyond realms of mind and matter
Keep your eye on the Ego
People immersed in their Ego can't get beyond it
Price too high to leave it
Unable to see on other side beyond the Ego
Spiritual attainments so high
Highest price must be paid
Your time, energy, separation from Ego
Barrier between Soul and remembering
Temporary illusion of separation
Sincere spiritual student gladly gives up
Time, attention, Ego, entire lower life
To attain this ocean of connection
Desire only Divine Beloved
Lower desires steeped in pain and separation
Seek connection with Divine Presence
Souls wants to step outside of time and matter
To experience union with Divine Essence
You have transcendent realities within you
Master Soul comes to remind you
You already have Divine qualities
Being called, time to remember
Spiritual liberation is freedom from your Ego
Mind enjoys playing in creation
Soul delights in creating and has creative power

Enchanted

When you jump into the Ocean of Divine Love
You will never leave
Completely content with infinite sea
You will spend the rest of your life

Trying to explain it to others
Most people are content with physical objects
You are the one in control of your spiritual life
A spiritual journey is to offer opportunity

Awareness that you are a Soul
Divine Being, a piece of Source
This higher reality can be real to you
Learn to step outside your Ego mind

Connect to your Higher Self, the Soul
You are a Divine Being in physical form
This life can swallow up all your attention
You get trapped in temporary illusion

Earth School has a lot to teach us
Don't get lost in recess, staying in playground too long
Mind seeks pleasures in physical realm
Soul desires truth of own identity

Oneness with Source
Mind causes identity theft
Whispers lies of only a human being
We are Divine Beings in human form

Journey to Glory

Work with your mind
Don't go into battle and fight
Your mind was made to think
Read spiritual material, enjoy relaxing music
Bring peace and calmness
Instead of discord and friction
Ego complains and is the enemy
Never wants to be reined in and controlled
Always wanting to roam free
Ego never wants to be held accountable for actions
How can you get anywhere with undisciplined mind?
Mind is difficult, not the journey
True spiritual teachers know this takes time
They are patient with their students
As a spiritual student continues on the journey
New perceptions and revelations
Integrated, embraced, accepted
Other Souls have earned spiritual attainments
You can succeed as well
Will be ups and downs
Connecting with Divine Presence
As you expand will gradually diminish
Causes consistent connection and awareness
Spiritual unfoldment never stops
Always expanding into infinity
Sometimes students feel the pace is too slow
Staying in exalted states takes time
Anything quickly gained is easily lost
Intensity needed for spiritual evolvement
A new way of life

Archangel

Many powerful archangels
Over the ages incarnated
Into human form
Without becoming famous
Serving a deeper level
Within humanity on Earth
Helping elevation of human consciousness
Higher Light Beings provide absolute service
They serve Divine Plan with strength
Perseverance through love and compassion
Archangels chose to be clothed in flesh
Service to humanity
Be aware of these Souls
Surrounding you with love
Here you are on this planet
Your Soul guides you in this life
You can tap into Divine Love
Available in every moment
Allow love that pervades to comfort you
Love is in everything
Even the tears and moments
When you feel alone
In the highest truth
You are never alone
Feeling of separation
Causes you to go within
Refuge of peace
Connect with your Soul
Greatest love is within
Nothing on the outer compares
You have great purpose
Your heart may have grown weary
On your journey never give up
Always the path of Divine Love to be found

Road to Majesty

Before all the religions
There was the Divine Essence
Created all the Souls

Going within offers awareness
Seeing our Divinity
Frees us from religious worship

Nothing compares, deep connection through Divine Love
Superpower of love brings you all the way back
To your home of origin

Spiritual ascension is only through
The power of love

Love is what comforts the heart
Controls the Ego
Governs the senses
Raises our states of consciousness
Brings us union

Divine Presence within
Stay connected through Divine Love
Power behind spiritual ascension

Pure Divine Love

Divine Presence goes before you
Will be always with you
Never will leave you
Always within you

Walking the journey alongside
Constant guidance when you ask
Have courage, remove doubts, never fear
You are never alone

Your footsteps are guided
Divine Love holds you
You are in a faraway land
Always with you

Reach out and I will hold your hand
Do not get discouraged
Feel me holding you close
I am with you always

You are made from My Essence
Pure Divine Love

Existence

A journey called mystic or esoteric
People unable to understand
Deep spiritual hidden mysteries
Try to understand with their mind
Ego is the barrier

Need to move beyond duality
Mind creates illusion
Awaken to unity consciousness
Experience the Oneness
Mind feels nothing is higher
Soul exclaims, "Soul Power!"

Your Soul understands wisdoms
Reality of Absolute realm
Soul sees through veil of illusion
Mind conceals the truth
Keeping mystery unsolvable

Slide Ego aside
Now sees through veil of illusion
True religion is discovering
True identity as a Soul
A piece of Source
You are a Divine Being

Horizon of Light

Be transformed, caterpillar to the butterfly
Divine Love has no restrictions
Humanity lives in the polarities of duality
Moving between two extremes constantly

Awakened person embraces Truth Consciousness
Moves toward unity and balance
Can spend life fighting the passions
Stay with indwelling Divine Presence

This love affair will bring you up
Your love will conquer these passions
Keeping you at evolved state of being

Let the passions play out
Don't spend all day drowned in them
It is your Ego that is getting upset

If you stay in your mind
You will forget your identity
You are this glorious Divine Being
Called the Soul

Spirited Shift

Once Soul incarnated into physical form
Took on the mind, it forgot its true identity
When able to see beyond the Ego
Can know true identity firsthand
Through direct mystical experience
Soul then remembers
Finds comfort in remaining time in physical form
What is being offered, much higher value
Than desire of objects in physical world
When mind tastes Divine Presence
Gladly surrenders, serves the Soul
In the beginning it seems fun
Until after a while
Begins to fade
Search for meaning happens
Path is within you
Stay with Divine Presence
Walk journey together
Communion is on the inner
Stepping onto a higher spiritual pathway
Causes awakening
Unawareness is dispelled
Oneness is seen
A person lives from the heart
Passage home is revealed
Home provides blissful love ambrosia
Never runs out, connect at any moment
Purpose for life illuminated
Know true identity
Service to Divine Plan
Soul desires Union with True Essence
Craves this joyous unification

Aurora

Your life can be a living walking meditation
Keeping your high state of being throughout the day
Causes this level of consciousness sustained
Ego gets tired of constant stress and disappointments
Soul awakens from Waking Nightmare
Sees all conundrums caused by Ego
Soul cleans up all situations
Holding one down to
Lower state of being
As our consciousness ascends
Impacts of blissful Divine Presence
Forever change the person's life
Realize you are in captivity of Egoic mind
Spiritual journey of Divine Love
Living from the heart, not intellect
Downloads and realizations keep coming in
Awakened remembering Divinity of the Soul
Mystical experience so profound
Divine Union experienced

Victory

Pathway is very broad, constantly expanding
Goal is liberation from mind and Ego
Barrier between Soul and Source
Mind makes us feel separate from Supreme Source
Soul feels separate while in human temple
Cannot be separate from what you are made of
Already One with Absolute Divine Source
Your mind is lying to you
Stop listening to the whispers of your Ego
Remember your Divinity with spiritual practices
Feel this bliss, love, companionship
Practicing the Presence means remembering
Divine Presence Within you
You begin experiencing total immersion
Divine Love rises from within
You have it already!
You just need to access it
Remember what you already are
A Pure Divine Essence
Talk with your Higher Self all day long
Best companion, truest friend, best counsel
Choose whom to be with all day, Ego or Soul
Trust me, Soul is the better choice
Soul always has highest interests for you
You need to tell your Ego
"Get off the throne!"
"My Soul needs a place to sit!"
Ego wants to hold tightly to rulership
Tell Ego to step aside so Soul can take control
Calm down all those stormy situations in life
Mastership keeps Ego in check
Soul custody of your attention
Ego loves drama, Soul provides true support
Enjoy peace, serenity, victory

World of Dreams

You are One with Infinite Absolute Being of Source
You existed before Earth was created
Part of One Divine Consciousness
Arrived on Earth for a purpose

Worth way beyond what you know
Came here to see beyond duality, this illusion
Let your personal story go, know your Divinity
Only a story experiencing in Waking Dream

Do you want peace?
Give up your personal story
Attachment to painful past
Move awareness to inner existence

As you walk through life
Never compare yourself to another
Soul sees no one greater or lesser
Only Ego creates these distinctions

Knowing Divinity with yourself and others
You see all ensouled and stand equally
Souls on journey of evolution and self-discovery

As a piece of Source, you are infinite
When you see your true identity
Only concerned with Oneness
While retaining your own unique individuality

Burden of a Blessing

You can be elevated to a higher level of consciousness
Travel in consciousness to higher dimensions
Consciousness can travel anywhere
Soul can reside on any plane of existence
Even in physical form can travel
To higher dimensions, experience spiritual attainments
Master Souls appear similar to you
Everyone must live in a body on physical dimension
They have reached a higher level of consciousness
These Souls can be talking with you
While living from God Realization state
They teach truth of Oneness
How Soul is the essence of Source
You are always with Source
Consciousness of Earth feels you here
You are Light expressed into form
Your vibrational frequency is felt
By animals and all of life on this planet
Light that you carry within is your power
You are the Light of the world
Everything is part of the One Expression of Source
We are the creation of Supreme Divine Essence
You are the Light of the Divine among humanity
Your essence is needed here on Earth
You emit high frequencies felt
Throughout this galaxy and beyond
When life gets overwhelming
Know you are on assignment
You will return to your home of origin
Never forget your importance
You are being prepared to be a Master Soul
Offering spiritual employment, positions to be filled
Destined to become colleagues of One Loving Source

Inner Light

You are already Self-Realized
You are already God Realized
Need to disassociate from your Ego
Staying in human consciousness
Hindering your spiritual ascent
True spiritual pathway is about remembering
True identity as a Soul
Who is a piece of Source

Divine Presence is within you and is you
You just don't believe it
As you spend more time
On a consciousness-expanding path

You will come to realize this truth
Merge your personal will with Divine Will
Free your Soul from bondage
Physical senses of outside world

Service to the Divine Plan
You are a spark of the Infinite Light
Revolutionary shift in consciousness to Oneness
Service to Source is service to all life

Strength and Honor

At some point in your spiritual journey
You will need to sacrifice everything
It is called your Ego Self
When you get to level where you can see it
Really see it in action
Ego knows it is on the radar
Ego can't hide anymore
On profound spiritual journey
Ego is tricky in the beginning
Ego causes problems to keep you off the pathway
While on the journey does not want to be controlled
Enemy on your transcendental path is your Ego
Separate entity can be your worst opponent
Ancient yogis mention power of Ego
Appendage to the Soul, navigates physical reality
When you are asleep, it helps you
When spiritually awakened, resists stepping aside
Let Soul rule all aspects of your life
High-level spiritual teachers tell you
A sacrifice needs to be paid
Ego to get tamed and calmed
At first Seeker feels sacrifice too much
Comes to realize is the ultimate freedom
Being free from antics of your Ego
Highest freedom you can experience in physical form
You know when Ego is stepping on Soul's toes
Trying to push Soul off the throne
Even after you reach your spiritual attainments
Keep an eye on the Ego
Knows when it is not being watched
Otherwise, Ego will be running your life
Life will have its ups and downs
You are not expected to be perfect
Only best efforts are required

Reminiscing Home

Aches so deep it is torturous
Gut-retching cries
There is no place like home
Service to the Divine Plan
Causes a sacrifice to leave
Home of origin dimension
Soul becomes homesick
Familiarity of Life
Anguishes for high resonance
Love Vibrational Frequency
Agony in lower realms
Humanity asleep in Waking Dream
Causes pain and suffering
To brother and sister Souls
What goes on in lower dimensions
Would never take place in higher realms
Lower vibrations unable to rise
Stay in darker more dense levels
Can go for visits
Internal connection obtainable
Upon arrival back
Creates longing for home origin
Just feeling of home
Brings bittersweet tears
Upon translation from this life
Enormous welcome back home
Mastership on your service
Formidable challenging assignment
Completion brings distinction

Higher Light Being

Never Back Down!
Take a break when needed
Adversary will try to conquer you
Every thought, emotion, outer situation
Lightworkers, hold your ground
You came here for this mission
Mass wakening now happening on Earth
Get into position for significant assignment
Lock in your powerful light
You have the power within you
Created from power of Source
You are a Higher Light Being for a spiritual war
Taking place on Earth presently
No place where Source is not
Source pervades everything
Ego distorted living in a corrupt world system
Now Lightworkers are waking up
Remembering their assignments
High-Frequency Light now coming to Earth
Darkness being cleared away
Lightworkers are boots on the ground
You walk among humanity
Keep your eye on goal and purpose work
Don't get lost in details of life
Can you see beyond your own life existence?
Humanity needs you, be unbreakable
Shine Your Light Brightly
You beam like the stars
Massive Powerful Divine Being
Never forget this
Temporarily a human being
Remember who you are and your power
When assignment completed
You will return back home
Walking off battlefield victorious
Battle scars show your service to Divine Plan

Spiritual Special Forces

Nothing is wasted in this life
When transition from this life
You will see much more fully
In order to be a spiritual general
You have to experience the battlefield
Earth University is extreme
High-level training and experience
On Spiritual Special Forces assignment
Your journey to glory
Yell your battle cry, pick up your sword, pierce darkness
Your mighty infinite light is more powerful than darkness
Dark world, that is why you came here
One of many here on this mission
Let Love of Source sustain you
Made of the One Source
You are a god in human form
Hold your head high
Powerful Divine Being
You came here to realize this
Had to step away temporarily
To understand more fully
Who you are and your power
Gods of Light from Supreme Infinite Light
Never Back Down from spiritual battle
You have this, regardless of appearances

Sacred Connection

Ego is like a spoiled child, wants everything
Does not care how it gets it, whom it hurts
Need to use love, other times instruction
Discipline Ego too harshly, will become rebellious
Use too much love, Ego will play with you
Still do what it wants, can't be too soft
Moderation and balance are required
Connect to Higher Self, ask what is needed
Develop this inner connection, daily dialogue
Journey can be treacherous, spiritual students need
Look for guide, mentor, teacher
Who has experience on this journey
Life will test us to see how well we are doing
Feel the love that is Within you
Your heart is beating, flow of your tears
Find love in your pain and sorrow
Find love when you are alone
Need to find strength to carry on
Your love can comfort others
You are never alone
Only appears this way
While in physical form
When you feel agony of disconnection
Will lead you to go Within
Peace can be found, experienced, greatest love
Sacred reconnection with your Soul
You have a great purpose
On the journey of Soul
Never give up when it grows dark
Stay connected, go within for Divine Guidance
You have it always with you
You are deeply loved and needed

Rise in Love

What makes spiritual journey intense?
Staying awake, aware constantly
Daily remember you are a Divine Being
In physical form having a human experience
Divine Presence is within you
Your Soul is a piece of Source
Makes you immortal, eternal, infinite
Let Love from your Soul come in
Get filled with this power
You are love in physical form
Rise in love with your Soul Self
Journey is knowing who you really are
Purpose being on spiritual pathway awakens you
Your true identity, achieve attainments
Transcending personal will to Divine Will
Perform service to the Divine Plan
Some people feel only down here to have a good time
You are in spiritual school and on assignment
Playground captures most attentions
Yes, can play, don't be consumed by it
Allow the Divine Beloved to pierce your heart
Profound tears are shed to put out intensity
Longing for union with the Divine
Tears help extinguish fire from pains of separation
Purification stage, preparation for higher-vibrational frequencies
Causes replacement of ego with Divine Presence
Soul is enraptured by the Divine Love
Mystical experiences cause absorption with Divine Source
Love of the purest form
Spontaneous tears uncontrollable, they just flow
Water helps with intensity of higher frequencies
On the sacred mystical journey

True Mastership

Master Soul Teacher will explain
Trying to get you into the water
When you finally go into the water
Will learn how to swim
Need instruction, learn information
Eventually student starts swimming
Mystical journey is experiential
Mind can only take you so far
Then steps aside so Soul can take over
Into higher levels beyond duality
Mental planes of existence
Master Souls know what is needed
An uphill journey
Spiritual attainments, very high accomplishment
Takes many years, like climbing a mountain
When needed, take breaks, then continue forward
You get to the top, will say worth time and effort
View from top of the mountain
Will change your perspective permanently
Master Soul Teacher is not the one
Who hands out the attainments
Self-Realization and God Realization are received
When your vibrational frequency reaches
A certain level that equals that attainment
That is how it works
Spiritual teacher is the guide and mentor
On this journey with you
They themselves spent years, sometimes entire life
Working on these attainments
Master Souls have reached Master Level
Have been asked to help other Souls
Who are ready for this journey
Spiritual attainments are beyond all teachings

There is no doctrine, no philosophy, no beliefs
Mastery of all three levels in cosmology
Physical plane, Emotional plane, Mental plane
Mastery of these levels is for the sincere student
If you want freedom from the Ego
Controlling you, your life, allow your Soul to rule
Master Souls are not any more special
They just got an earlier start
Are further along, are here for service
Master Souls know eventually students
Will reach mastery depending upon
Effort put forth, sincerity, and receptivity
Spiritual journey is to transfer from
States of consciousness to Oneness
The I AM pure consciousness
No end to expansion of your consciousness
Will spend eternity expanding, serving Divine Plan
Your love for Supreme Essence will be so great
You will spend eternity being in service
Higher one goes, more they serve
With great love, Source's Divine Plan
We are talking about true Mastership, Divine Connection

Divine Love Frequency

When you leave your physical form
You go to vibrational level achieved in consciousness
Untold levels on the other side
Dimensions upon dimensions
All based upon vibrational frequencies

Many Souls on Earth working on consciousness expansion
Attainment of spiritual goals
Understanding spiritual energetic law of vibrational frequencies
Do you want to reside at vibrational level with
Master Souls and supreme Hierarchs?

I suggest sorting out what is really important to you
Something you can carry beyond this life
Everything stays behind except your spiritual accomplishments
All in Cosmic University moving up through levels
Many extremely high-level Souls incarnated on Earth

We all have to pull rotation for the lower grades
We came here to help those who got lost along the journey
Came to help others wake up from Waking Dream
Crossing the veil into physical dimension wipes our memory

Our intense light and vibrational frequency
Help in causing mass awakening on this planet
Many highly evolved master-level Souls
Are on assignment here in service to other Souls
Supreme Hierarchs call Source, Divine Love Frequency

Beyond the Ego

Trying to walk entire spiritual journey by your mind
Won't work, mind can only take you so far
Journey takes you beyond your Ego
How is it going to help you when reach that point?

A level where mind has to step aside
Only Soul can go forward
Self-Realization and God Realization
Beyond mental realms

Mind is dual in nature
Nonduality realms above mind power
Many spiritual students plateau
Cannot figure out with their mental power

Self-Realization and God Realization attainment
A journey you surrender your Ego mind complex
In order to get beyond it
Mind can't take you there

Journey is being intoxicated by love of Infinite Source
Union, Oneness, bliss, absorption, freedom

Energetic Sovereignty

Self-Realization your goal?
Ego cannot remain in primary position
Soul can escape from control of Ego

When experienced seeing itself in pure form
No body, ego, personality, shadow self
All removed, only pure energetic essence seen

During mystical experience of Self-Realization
Nothing compares seeing your true identity
Energetic sovereignty of your Soul

Realization of your True Self
Once experienced Self-Realization
Can never go back to old identity

Forever transformed, liberated from Egoic mind
Ego serves you while in physical form
Your True Self is ruling your universe

Grand Overall Design

Spiritual student's goal
Attain God Realization
Accept spiritual assignment
All highly evolved Souls given mission before incarnating
When they arrive, get lost in the circus of life
Expected in beginning, need to adjust down here
Experience life in physical world
A time comes to awaken, remember goals, purpose work
When remember their assignment
Some Souls feel overwhelmed
Feel heavy responsibility
Much being asked of them
These Souls need encouragement to step out
Start serving Divine Will instead of personal will
Many of you are Starseeds from higher realms
You came here for service
Must become adept, like other Master Souls
Who came before you on this planet
This is what is being offered to you
When you attain God Realization
Plenty of spiritual positions to be filled
In service to Divine Plan
Grand Overall Design for this universe

Mastership Level

All paths ultimately lead a person
To journey of Self-Realization and God Realization
May take several lifetimes
When they are ready, journey will be exposed to them

All paths are stepping stones for evolving consciousness
In Earth School, every Soul learning at different level
Master Soul instructors teach Souls ready
Ultimate goal to reach Mastership level

Students who reach attainments handed spiritual assignments
Spiritual assignments come from higher realms
Master Souls know need to be replacements
One day teacher leaves the planet

Soul's attainment is service at higher level
Showing Divine Reality within
Soul's reason for existence

Appropriate validation to be fully qualified
Leads to deeper level of service
To Source's Divine Plan

Deeper Degree

Once you receive spiritual bliss
Of Divine Love, nothing else matters
This love so powerful, Soul wants to stay
Absorption of Divine Presence within you

You still live in outside world
Recognize inner more real than outer world
Have traveled their realms within
Know difference between the two

A Realized Person still has difficulties
They provide ability to transcend them
Sees these as temporary circumstances
Let people live out their lives

Allow things to run their course
You cannot change another person
Only they can change themselves
They have to do their own inner work

Be happy your awareness is high enough
Seeing value in expanding your consciousness
Stay close to Divine Presence
Know this power is Within you

A Realized Soul

A Realized Soul cares little for the world
Will play their role, complete assigned mission
A Realized Soul is always ready
To return to their home of origin

Back to where they resided
Prior to this physical incarnation
They have no attachment to this world
It is very temporary

Realized Souls accomplish their assignments
To the best of their abilities
Master Souls look forward to the day
They get to translate, leave physical dimension

Remember their Family of Light
Cannot wait to be reunited with them
Fulfilled their service to Divine Plan
Continue to serve on other future assignments

Some days can be hard for them here
They remember and visit while sleeping
Dimensional level they came from prior
To accepting this assignment on Earth

Excitement of Reuniting

When you get tired of the circus of life
Will start looking for a highly evolved spiritual teacher
Who can help you reunite with Oneness
Will reconnect with Family of Light
Talk about a celebration
You cannot imagine it until direct experience
Enormously vast celebration
Everyone from dimensional origin level
Comes for this excitement of reuniting
Love flows along with the music
Never heard on Earth before
Sheer bliss experienced
When a Soul gets back home
Then you are Realized
When you come back down to Earth
To complete your assignment
Physical dimension seems dull in comparison
Reason why Realized Souls
Don't care for this world much
Spend time connecting to a higher reality
They perform their daily duties, purpose work
Their hearts are attached to
Divine Presence within them

Expansion

You are welcome to stay down
In lower dimensions until
You get tired of all the circus rides
After a while Soul wants to return home
In the end, you decide when you are ready
Evolutionary journey toward realization
Return to your home of origin
Wise spiritual student realizes
Mind cannot deliver complete utter happiness
You have to go to a higher realm
Beyond mental powers of mental dimensions
When you feel loneliness
Your Soul is homesick
Mind thinks needing outward company
When you lie down to sleep
Body needs rest
Soul never sleeps
Many nights are journeys into other dimensions
Reason you don't remember them
Visiting realms beyond the mind
Sometimes you wake up more tired
Your consciousness is nonlocal
You can be everywhere simultaneously
Your Soul is a piece of Source
Has power of being omnipresent
Being present in all places
Offers ability for night travels
Soul requires experiences for expansion

Remarkable

Spiritual Seeker, you are a rare individual
Exceptional level of consciousness
Uncommon to general population
You are remarkable in your quest
Upward movement in consciousness
Have come to realize your life
Needs to be more than being centered
Around your Ego and personality
Eager for spiritual truths
Answer mystery of life
You know there are spiritual wisdoms
Deep longing starts the search
Further along the journey
There are pains of separation
Journey eventually brings you to attainments
Self-Realization and God Realization
Spiritual journey is about spiritual truths
You will move to stage of surrender
Yield your personal will to Divine Will
Spiritual life focus service to Divine Plan
Will naturally be attracted to Union and Bliss
To become Realized Souls is rare
See highly coveted attainments
Having significant worth
Allowing Soul to awaken
Spiritual power to control egoic mind
Great treasure to Souls who realize
Attainment of spiritual goals
Offers spiritual potential and mastery

Exploration

A true pathway will help you
Differentiate between truth and illusion
Absolute truth and relative truth
Soul and mind
Divine Will and Personal Will
Elevate from human consciousness
To transcendental spiritual consciousness
You are not alone in your quest
Many looking for deeper meaning
Very little seems to satisfy them anymore
Start their search for spiritual truths
A Master Soul has compassion for human condition
Most Souls don't know about their Divine Nature
Much less how to navigate Egoic mind
When in their Ego or connecting with Higher Self
Spiritual mastery similar from child becoming an adult
Exploration, many experiences occur before adulthood
Spiritual journey, time, effort, growing experiences
Spiritual Mastership requires ardent training
Ego and personality are temporary
Need to distinguish between
Soul and mind, inner dimensions
Awareness of illusory conditions
Desire Mastership
Master your own cosmology
Thoughts, emotions, subconscious imprints, actions

Splendor

Master Soul will teach to know real from unreal
You can become a Spiritual Master in this life
Available to you and can be achieved
Highest ideal in human form

Your Soul can experience rarified higher states
A spiritual journey offers ability to experience
Eternal, nameless, formless, limitless, everlasting
Majestic, permanent, glorious, celestial essence

Human body called human temple
If only you knew your own essence
Opportunity to experience true identity
While you are living in physical form

Advanced spiritual journey will liberate you
Barrier, controlling effects of the mind
You want freedom to become a Master Soul
In your own divine right

When you are ready, will be attracted to start
Spiritual journey into these divine mysteries
Natural affinity created between student and teacher
Soul is same essence as Beloved Supreme Source

Who is really calling you?
Beloved is calling you back home
To remember and reunite
You have just forgotten, that's all
I am reminding you of your identity

Celestial Essence

Soul is already pure, is a piece of Source
No difference between Soul and Source
Issue is coverings over the Soul
Mental body, thoughts
Astral body, emotions
Physical body, actions
Causes barriers for the Soul
To have conscious union
With Divine Presence
We have the connection
Coverings cause constraints
Making people feel there is separation
True Self is really what you want to meet
Seeing actual Soul Essence becomes the quest
To know who we really are
When all the coverings are removed
Realization of True Self is
Self-Realization of our Divinity
Soul cannot rise to surface beyond coverings
Without Egoic mind causing struggle to keep control
A spiritual journey that challenges the Ego
It can be a spiritual battle
Mind will fight the Soul
Eventually, Egoic mind becomes spiritualized
In harmony with Soul
Surrender of Ego comes and serves Soul
Raising of energies causes awakening
Purification of ego, emotions, personality, shadow, physicality
Once Soul in complete control over mind
Body Consciousness transcended
Personal Will serves Divine Will

Majestic Power of Soul

Your true identity is within
Most people think their identity
Is in the outer world
Self-exploration, significant part of journey
You need to know who you are first
In order to understand who you are not
True identity is Soul
False identity is Ego
Part of enlightenment process
Becoming enlightened in truth
We are all Divine Beings
Know real from unreal
Soul is real, permanent, infinite
Ego and personality are unreal
Aspects of mind and temporary
When you leave your physical form
Ego and personality formed in present lifetime
Stay connected to time track for each incarnation
Divine Source and Soul are permanent
Real because omnipresence, omnipotence, omniscience
Anything dual in nature or distinction
Mind, thought waves, mental powers
Soul is beyond dimensions of duality
Soul is generating power of the mind
Mind cannot function without
Majestic power of Soul
Soul can exist on its own
Soul is a piece of Infinite Source

Real from Unreal

Truth is eternal
Untruth is temporary
Truth is infinite
Untruth is filled with illusion

Identification with thought waves
Causes distortion of our identity
You are a Soul
Identification with anything else

Unreal, temporary in this life
Once Self-Realization attained
No longer identify with
Outer, unreal, temporary world

Your true identity is energetic
Beyond all aspects of mind
You are not your mind, mental powers
If you stay with your mind all day

Will identify with unreal, mistaken image
Stay with your true identity, Soul
Keeps you in higher perspective of life
You are navigating Real from Unreal

Magnetic

No one can take away
What is in your destiny
Your Higher Self
Will give you everything
Have firm faith

Worldly obligations you are fulfilling
All essentially spiritual
Everything is working in your favor
Regardless of appearances
Nothing is wasted

All experiences are spiritual training
When you walk off
Spiritual battlefield of your life
You are proud of all the battle scars
You accumulated in this lifetime

Go through your day remembering
You are a Divine Being
Your connection with Source
Always love upon you

As you go through your day
You just have to tap into it
Your consciousness will merge
Into that which you love

Glorious

Grace is always there
You will become strong
You have it already within you
Have no fear
We are connected as One

We all come from
Great One Infinite Source
Source already in saints and humanity
Only difference is that ordinary person
Unawake has veil of Ego

Separates them from knowing
True identity of being a piece of Source
Concept until a person has mystical experience
Self-Realization and God Realization
Fortunate to have Master Souls on Earth

Humanity requires high-vibrational energy
To counterbalance all negativity in human collective
We are all walking gods as Divine Beings
Stay in constant connection with highest power
Source will be with you wherever you go

Walking Divinity

Beloved will do whatever is for your benefit
No one can erase what is in your destiny
No one can have what is meant for you

Free Will also plays a role in your life
Destiny and Free Will cause certain experiences
Humanity can meet Divine Presence regardless of status or beliefs
Saints have taught Divine Source is within us

Divine Presence beyond mind and intellect
Move beyond lower dimensions
Physical, mental, emotional planes
To experience Oneness, Realization of Self

God Realization is existing within
You are Walking Divinity
All Souls, from all countries, races
Like flowers of different colors in same garden

All living on same planet, under same sky
Dividing ourselves into groups, imprisoned ourselves in them
Master Soul Teacher's objective to free humanity
From cage of Egoic mind and body

World is a dream, only temporary
Mind causes the dream, wants it to continue
Purification of the mind, removes the veil
Seeing the Oneness and Divine Essence

Temple of Light

All different belief systems getting light
From same Supreme Candle
Realized Souls are full of love for the Divine
Have affection for all of creation

Take the journey providing inner experience
Directly see inner dimensions, Divine Essence
One thing told, quite another to have personal experience
Self-discovery, essence of spirituality

You are so connected
Hardwired to Source
Divine pervades whole universe
Stillness inside always there

Can enter stillness within whenever we wish
You are a drop of Source
There is no you, only Source
Pervades all and IS everything

About you coming to know who you are
A part of Source Light
Always remember, dear Soul
You do not belong to this world

Divine Dance

When you realize everything is Source
You entrust everything to Beloved Supreme Essence
All becomes Source
You are made of Source

Walking human temple
Because of what is inside you
This world is lowest and most miserable of all
As we go to higher realms, enjoy more happiness

No peace in this world
Peace is within us
Have to go beyond physical dimension
I gave up my life that I knew before

Now my life is no longer mine
Surrendered to the Beloved
Thy Will Be Done now
Supreme Beloved has important plans for you

Let nothing sidetrack you
Keep love and harmony among yourselves
You are very useful in the hands of
Divine Presence in doing this very good work

Tranquility

Do not worry about detachment
As you get into these higher-vibrational states
All attachments fall away
Don't use mental acrobatics to cause changes
Leave all that alone

Focus on achieving higher states of consciousness
When you arrive there, they fall away naturally
You lose interest in them
You can take them or leave them
Focus on raising your frequency

Will cause situations to change
Some attachments will stay, some will leave
Honoring highest and best for you
Higher Self knows what is needed and not needed
Trust this internal guidance within you

There is a Homecoming Welcome Banquet
You are the guest of honor
Everyone in your dimension of origin
Waiting for your return home

Divine Days

There is no greater wealth
Than progress on the spiritual journey
Wealth that accompanies us even after death

Spiritual journey based on spiritual love
Seeker comes to see love is life stream
Elixir of Love keeps life in full bloom
Go beyond the Ego, drink from the cup of love

On the path of love, one has to be sincere
Quest of Self-Discovery, reconnection
Inner relationship with Supreme Beloved
Divine Presence becomes the Lover of such lovers

Spiritual love is such an intense intoxication
Takes us above the physical world
Causes inner mystical experience, being with Beloved
Source is Love, Soul is made from Source

Love is a fire that burns away
All evil tendencies from egoic mind
Moment it is awakened

Beloved will say to you
"You are the only one in my eyes"
When Soul is touched by the Beloved
Constant flow of the stream of love

Ultimate Testing

This density provides valuable experience
Very important school, test-drive for trillions of Souls
Earth School provides most extreme
Toxic conditions to test, lessons, continue evolution

Density so thick, suffocating
Crossed the veil, entered into this incarnation
Lost your memory of other dimensions
Starting to awaken, remember your true identity
Protect yourself from low-vibrational frequencies

High spirituality is required to stay awake and aware
Several large Absolute Cosmic Universities
Send their Starseed students to Earth
For ultimate testing and training
Spiritual Green Beret training for next assignment

In service to the Divine Plan
Lower the dimension, greater the density
Toxicity, hatred, greed, cruelty
More valuable experience Soul can master
You are in process of becoming a saint

Saint sees the Creator everywhere
Saints sees life differently
Consciousness elevated and purified
You are on the journey to sainthood
Start practicing this lifestyle
Live the spiritual life

Endurance

Fortunate to hear of
Self-Realization, God Realization attainments
Rare that a person proceeds to pursue them
Rarer to achieve Self-Realization, God Realization
These attainments require tenacity
Journey causes you to walk through difficult landscapes
When you are in love with Truth
You are in love with pathway to Divine through Truth
This love causes Seeker to transcend the Ego
Become friendly with your Ego
Ego needing a friend to help it
Becomes agreeable with service to Soul
Spirituality about overcoming selfishness
Conversion of Ego to be of service to Higher Self
You want to reach advanced state of being?
Need to transcend duality of this or that
Us against them mentality, duality causes separation
You want to dissolve the opposites
Spirituality, new way of being in the world
This world is the grit that polishes
You into a diamond
This world brings forth bravery
Courage, stamina, determination
Fortitude, endurance, tolerance
Earth School is evolution of consciousness
Service to the Divine Plan
People who are so high vibrationally
Counterbalance negativity of human collective

A Diamond

Society rests on spiritual progress
Realization of the Soul leads to happiness
Without the Soul, body of no use

No spiritual progress, then as a result
Intolerance, selfishness, sectarianism
Narrow-mindedness, bigotry prevail
Causing hatred and disputes among various groups
Source is the treasure among various groups
Source is the treasure of all powers

This power is within us
Connect internally and gain strength
Since our Soul is a piece of Source
Soul has great strength
A Diamond has brilliance and value

If you cover a diamond with mud, not lost value or shine
You may not see the sheen
Wash it, will see original brilliance and value
When Soul is placed into physical form
Taken on a covering, lost appearance of brilliance

Then comes a mystic who shares of true identity
Revealing our true identity as Divine Souls
Removes coverings of their Egoic mind
Soul's brilliance and value are visible

You and Source

Lightworkers, Watchful Guardians of Earth
You came here to be in human form
Earth is very dense and dark
This is why you came here
Now you see why
Very important mission for you
Guardians needed among human collective
When you get overwhelmed by dark corruption
Remember who you are, why you are here
If you see yourself as broken
You have forgotten your true identity
I am here to remind you
Dear Lightworker, you are
In service to the Divine Plan
I know that your heart aches
You hurt, miss your home dimension
Prior to incarnation on Earth
Stay strong, stay encouraged, stay on track
Keep moving forward, your light needed here
Find community of other Lightworkers
This will help you
You will look back
Not feel this life was wasted
You will see after translation from life
How much you have helped
You said you wanted to be tested
Lightworker, remember this is really
Between You and Source

Spiritual Progress is Earned

When you really understand
Beloved always with you
Remembrance comes
Spiritual journey is not straight up the mountain
Moments when pathway is unpredictable
Journey will be intense, spiritual passion, devotion
Times when you will sacrifice everything
At times experience a plateau
Master Soul Teacher will know
There are times spiritual growth so quick
Feels like an avalanche, drowning in it
Expansion coming in so fast
Times you experience spiritual dryness
You come to a level where you have
No dependence on continual experience
Spiritual visions, no out-there-ness
All reality is the Oneness
Reality of the Whole
You experience your Divinity Within
No longer requiring experience, you know
When completed lessons, goals, attainments
You have permission to leave
Come to a realization
Once you reach a high level
Your force benefits life on Earth
You leave or go is immaterial
Stay in physicality, benefit life
You are already here
Will be periods of seclusion
Living monastic lifestyle, inner work
Quiet space to achieve spiritual attainments
Then you step out, take your assignment
Service to the Divine Plan

Spread This Light

When you have a close friend
Are separated from them
Anxious to be with them again
People who are filled with love
Connection with Source

Filled with love for Divine Essence
They have a longing and yearning
To go back home
These are the blessed ones
When Soul gets released from Ego

Peace is obtained, become Self-Realized
You can live at peace within yourself
Radiate peace around yourself
Share peace with others
Public may cause you heartache
Human collective focused on outward

Your way is inward
Try not to worry how world treats you
You are in good company, my friend
Many saints, prophets, Master Souls
Mistreated by the world

Lightworker, don't underestimate
Your light within yourself
Wherever you go in this world
You will Spread this Light

Energy of Soul

Experiencing separation causes you to
Seek union and Oneness
With Divine Presence within yourself
Union and Oneness come
When your heart is filled with Divine Love
There is no you
There is only Source
That piece of Source is your Soul
See how important you are?
Your personal sense of identity
Ego and personality
You are a Divine Being
In physical form having human experience
Living to the will of your Egoic mind
That is not living at all
When you live by Divine Will
You have no will of your own
Risen above the realm of mind
Light shines in the darkness
Ego prevents light from Soul to shine
Ego barrier between Soul and Source
Ego lowered, connection, Oneness
Darkness is an illusion
When light shines, darkness disappears
Eliminate this veil of darkness
Realize Divine Source within
Soul within shines when darkness removed
Inner Light and Sound, Energy of Soul

Living Dead

Who are the living dead?
Those who have forgotten the Divine
They are living in the world

So deeply have forgotten
True identity as a Divine Being
One day, these people will hear

Voice of the Divine
Become filled with love
Serve the Divine Plan

Secret Garden

Divine Souls
Pretending to be
Mere mortals in
Secret Garden of Earth
You have Soul Power
Flowers in this world
Sing to you, dear Soul
Only your Soul can hear
Sweet melodies for you
Earth is a garden
Souls to experience
This physical life
All of creation exclaims
Divine Souls Awake!
Sleep no more
Time to remember
Your Divine Magnificence
Garden of Earth
Only temporary
A necessary visit
Absolute Spectacular Realm
Awaits you upon return Home

Life Force

An Awareness
Seeker after Truth
I AM, the Awareness
Many identities on the outer
Notice your situation
Mind is afraid of the heart
Heart says, "Take it all"
Mind says, "Wait a minute"
Egoic world wants you
To remain a separate entity
Awareness shows Oneness
Secret is to handle the balance
Between Mind and Heart
Compassionate Heart, Logical Mind
Can keep a balance without closing either one
Don't close yourself off
Life Force of the Universe
Get back to Source
Get back to unity, Oneness
Wake up from the Waking Dream
Living in the world
Experience beyond this world
You become formless
Become form then return
Back into the formless
In the highest reality
You are form and formless together
Spirit and human simultaneously
Behind the mind is Awareness
Pain and pleasure
Happiness and suffering
Awareness is beyond duality
Learn to balance
You are spirit in form

Paradox

Patterns of energy
In form and without form
You exist in more than one reality
Reality of thoughts
Reality of emotions
Reality of actions
Reality of Awareness
Your Higher Self
Goal is to be free
Only the Soul has freedom
Higher Self sees suffering
Part of the human experience
Suffering and Bliss both exist
Spiritual wisdom shares
Universe is perfect and tragic
Acceptance of what is
Both are true, both exist
Perfection in human experience journey
Being free from the mind
True Freedom
Agony and ecstasy
In the same universe
Acceptance brings balance
Paradox of the universe

Light Ambassador

Your consciousness is infinite
You live in power
Resonating with Frequency of Source
You became human to experience

The dream, duality, then return to Oneness
Desiring Soul experience
You became human
Life is working for you

You are safe
This world is not your destination
You are a creator being
Powerful to make changes in your life

Your life is your contribution to this world
You are a Soul, Pure Source Energy
Divine Absolute Source created
All seen and unseen realms

All energies and all frequencies
Source Light flows throughout
All the galaxies and universes
We are Lights of the Great Light

You are a Light Ambassador
Light up the Earth
Bring forth love and joy
Connection with Sacred Source Frequency

Walking Temple of Source

You hold Power of Source Energy
Shift conceptual reality to True Reality
Consciousness is resonating as different forms
Soul has Omnipresent quality
Ultimate nonlocal field is consciousness

You are energy, eternal, infinite
Your DNA and body emit Light
Unique expression of Source
Source experiencing Itself
In many disguising forms

Being an aspect of Source
You are Immortal, Eternal, Source Essence
Walk through life knowing all is Source
Seeing the Divine in All
You are a Walking Temple of Source

You exist because of Source's love for you
You are Source and Source is you
It's all Source and thus Oneness
You are a Divine Being
No one is more powerful than you

Made in the image of Source
All that exists is Source's Essence
Soul is a piece of Source
Remember your True Identity
Soul has everything you need

Love Potion

I sipped your love potion,
Was never the same.
Now I see you everywhere,
Lovesick for you.

I am drunk on the wine
From the Divine.
Don't wake me up,
Please be so kind.

Dreamed of bliss
And happiness.
Love elixir cleanse the Soul,
Two united became whole.

Soul and Beloved

I've come back for you, my dear one.
Don't be fooled by the world of appearances.
Love has come to take you home.
If you see anything other than love, that is not real.
My wish for you is to see through
and beyond all this matter, space, time.
Your body is on loan; one day,
you'll be free of the mind and emotions.
All that is you is Soul, a drop of the Divine.
I know who you are.
Your Source is calling you back home.
Do you know how fortunate you are
to be able to talk to this Powerful Essence?
Come to know of my secret.
Throw off these coverings, reveal the Pure Soul.
Where illusion exists, thought must exist.
Spell of illusion, temporary separation
of Soul from Divine.
Where there is only the Divine, no thought can exist.
Illusion and Thought
Soul and Beloved
Thought breaks our connection
Mind keeps you in illusion
Soul, stay close, don't forget about me today.
Watch the thoughts, stay on the path of love and devotion.
This is just a play down here; let go of all anxieties,
come and live in my world
of peace and bliss.

Soul Vs. Mind

Mind creates Drama
Soul bathes in Peace
Mind causes Separation
Soul swims in Harmony
Mind sends deception, distortions
Soul already Pure
Mind full of Personality
Soul radiates Love
Mind manifests Logic, Reason, Illusion
Soul has Direct Perception
Mind wants Control
Soul enjoys being Happy
Mind's Ego is Angry
Soul is a Blissful entity
Mind, Temporary expression
Soul, Eternal Spark
Mind creates illusion
Soul has Secured Freedom
Mind manifests External stimuli
Soul possesses External attributes
Mind experiences tension, separation, conflict
Soul understands Knowing, Being, Seeing
Mind, drowning in Negativity
Soul, drop from Divine Ocean
Mind, controlled by Universal Mind Power
Soul, Essence of Supreme Source

Becoming You

Stepped into the World
Forgot my True Self
Identity Theft
Being with the Mind
Endless Games
True Identity Appears
Love Floods the Soul
Purifies All Bodies
Truth will become You
Constant Communion
Identity with Source
Switched Identity
Became You
Realization of Oneness

Purification

What did I do to deserve the love of the purification?

Knowing the Divine is in me provides the strength to endure.

Love from the Divine is the purification.

Divine Love is so powerful, it burns away all the impurities.

Intensity of this love creates the heat that burns.

Heat of desire fuels the fire of love more,
as the intensity picks up toward the Divine.

Pleasure of pain is understood when the karmas are paid in full.

The agony of separation turns to full joy
when the purification is complete.

How blessed indeed is the one going through
the purification journeys.

Next to You

Why do you feel alone?

When have I told you,
you are alone?

This feeling is fleeting,
comes and goes.

Can't you see me,
next to you,
looking into your eyes?

Beautiful one,
special one,
how can I ever
forget you?

You are made from
the essence of myself.

I loved you before
heavens were created.

How can I forget myself?

Singing to You

How can one live this earthly life?
When the Divine is nearby.

How can one continue in this dream?
When the Divine is blowing you kisses to wake you up.

This is no earthly love
beyond frontiers, my dear.

The stars are even jealous of how
the Divine pays so much attention to you.

Hear the Divine singing to you?
Divine's love call is so enchanting.

The music gets louder and louder
until the Love wins you over.

Don't fight too hard, let the Divine have you.
This is the deepest love.

Be happy the Divine is chasing you.

Transcended

Walking with the Divine
Effects One Deeply
Outside Noises, Disturbances
Social Daily Life
Pain of Separation
Nearly too much to bear

Going deeper inward
Remaining in Samadhi
Staying connected
Focused with the Beloved
Saturated with Love
United with Source

Acceptance of Life
Human Consciousness Transcended
Deeper Understanding
Earthly Existence
Commissioned Mission
You signed up

Samadhi focused State
Perfect for Source Plan
Stepped down the Power
While stationed here
Present Spiritual Ecstasy
Service to the Divine Plan

Your Gift

You are Special
One of a Kind
Uniquely Created
Eternally Divine

Before Incarnation
Talent Imprinted
Guidance Selected
Sent from Above

Encouragement Continued
Inspiration Required
Contemplate Fulfillment
Confirmation is Laughter

Inner Beingness
Creativity Abounds
You will Know
Energy will Flow

Oneness

Oneness, Inner Space
Oneness, Outer Space
Interconnected, Selected
Totally Unified

Soul's Indivisible Oneness
Look for the One
That teaches Oneness
We are many, yet One

One in Origin, Came from Divine
One is Design, One of a Kind
Let's cry together, Laugh together
Ultimate Goal, One with Divine

This world teaches us
Living on same planet together
Each unique path, same journey
Steps toward Home

Soul started as One, in Higher plane
On Planet Earth, became many identities
Soul sheds lower appendages
Rises upward to its Divine Oneness

Divine Union

Stop screaming Mind!

Soul craves Divine Union

Stop creating Drama

Soul wishes for Serenity

Stop talking

Soul requests Quietness

Quit Yelling!

Soul requires Divine Connection

Stop looking around

Walk your own path

Inner Path, Inner Union

Divine Union

Pierce the Veil

See beyond the Veil
of duality
of relationships
of belief systems

What is beyond
this Veil
this matrix
this hologram

Love pierces
Love exposes
Love teaches
Love reveals

First see the Veils
Lift each Veil
Rise above
Unveiling your True Self

Duality

Pain and Pleasure
Duality is the teacher
Look for the lessons
Both sides reside inside

Starts out as a rainy day
Turns into a sunny day
Look for the rainbow
Shows light through water droplets

Dirt and Darkness
Seeds and Sunlight
Create the canvas
Duality creates life

Extreme ends of the same pole
These emotions inside you
Experienced in dual nature
Show both are you

You are both darkness and light
Human experience provides this truth
Now, rise Above Duality
Your higher identity is Divine

Sacrifice

Sacrifice my body, mind, emotions
in order to be with you

Provide me with your inner Presence
You are what sustains me

Life is a wasteland without you
everywhere I look are the passions

How can I go on without you?
Now that we have met

Restore me with the Divine Presence

Flow of tears
Fires of longing
Connecting daily
Distraught with anguish

I now understand Divinity

Personal life is over
All about the Divine Plan
All-consuming love
Surrendered my life for you

Ocean of Tears

Let the tears cleanse my Soul

Wash away the impurities, the pain

Deep aches, grieving of being away from you

Never felt pain go so deep

When will my Soul be in union with the Divine?

Painful yearning, process of cleansing

Wash me pure of all karmas

Crying an ocean of tears for you

Nothing satisfies this Soul

Beloved holds the key to my heart

Come quickly and be with me

You've turned up the volume of the sphere-music

Loudspeakers in my ear

Your Love Call tells me you are nearby

Bring us toward Union

When you become One with the Divine, there is no you

All that you do disappears, Divine becomes the Doer

Courting with Delight

Beloved, you speak to me day and night,
You are courting me with delight.

You see the tears flow down my face,
I hear the words, filled with grace.

You know me deeply,
Sing to me sweetly.

Your love is sincerely true,
Sweet perfume is all around you.

When the Divine Melody is heard,
Experiencing the Word.

Destiny

The road that you must travel
was in the stars before you came

Every step preordained
you feel drawn to a higher life

You are known, beautiful Soul
reaching out for your hand

Come to higher regions
It's your Destiny

You are meant to be with me
Release, trust me

Beyond the veil
you will see me
waiting for you

Transformation awaits you
It's your Destiny
to be united with me

Stars foretell of Destiny
At one point, you will become me

Holding Hands

I saw you today, Beloved,
holding tightly my hand.

Experiencing your love,
tears flowing down,
overwhelming me.

Sending a message,
"You are my very own,
truly know that you are loved."

Dazzling lights catch my eyes,
forgetting my Beloved.

Remember, Remember,
Grabbing the Beloved's hand once again,
now in tune with the melody.

Run Quickly

Language of Love
is intimate connection
with Divine to Soul

Birds love to be with the sky
Trees deep connection with the earth

Keep an open ear
to the Divine's enchanting melody

Body does not know how to handle
the Soul crying out
to be with the Divine Essence

It is time to break free
Run Quickly
before the mind wakes up
follow the music
the audible life stream
your deepest friend

Ocean of Love and Mercy
is waiting for the drop

Continue on the river
that takes you to the ocean

Late-Night Date

Date with Divinity
Oh, how sweet!

Smelled the Divine
Love perfume all around

Mind was dizzy
Ego was spinning

Soul was dancing
With delight

Could not sleep
Seeing the Divine's gaze

Spent the evening
Talking with the Presence

Enjoy these
Loving eyes
Upon me

Living Image

Divine is a Living Image
Let's stay together
Constant connection
In daily life

Splendor moments of
Love Waves washing over me
Brings tears, seeing you near

Your loving eyes
Gazing into mine
Washing impurities away
Purification with Love

Hold on to what is True
Hold on to what is Real
Release illusion, confusion

Temporary images hold one down
Gravity to the Soul
Come up to higher ground
The Living Image

Sing to the Divine

A sparrow was singing in a tree when a Mystic Saint came walking by. The bird sang out and asked the Mystic, "Please stay for a while."

The Mystic so full of love and grace responded, "Sing to the Divine."

The bird sang the sweetest song. Mystic Saint's eyes were wide. The sparrow felt a love wave go through her. She had never experienced this before and fell out of the tree.

The Mystic Saint caught her gently.
Her love for the Mystic Saint began to grow.
The Mystic Saint was a Divine Being, not like all the others. With a smile, the Mystic sat down under the tree with the sparrow on his palm. She was so happy her heart felt as if it would burst from all the love.

The sparrow realized that the Mystic was indeed Divine in the flesh! Amazing gift to be in the Divine's hand. Love songs came constantly, and even her voice changed. She vowed to spend her life always thinking of Source. All her songs would be sung to the Living Presence. Every action would be for her Beloved. Her life was no longer her own; it now belonged to the Divine.

The Living Presence continued to gaze at her and enjoy her songs to the Divine. Then the Mystic leaned down and whispered sweetly in her ear, a promise in her future life.

She sang so loud and hopped onto the Saint's shoulder. The sparrow would spend the rest of her days with the Mystic Saint. This Master Soul would always have her nearby singing to provide companionship.

Her life would never be the same, for she was forever changed.

Marked

Marked Soul,
you are blessed.

Came for you,
please stay near,
you are forever dear.

Life is a shadow,
pay no mind.

Focus on connection,
one day resurrection.

Whispers in your ear,
my great love for you.

Kisses on your forehead,
wake you up at night.

Who is courting you?

Your forgotten Source.

Missing you, time to come Home,
leave the playground, physical friends,
dance with me all the way Home.

Union with Sound

That Divine Melody
constantly rings in my ear.

The ringing radiance
I will forever hear.

The voice of the Divine
singing sweetly is sublime.

How can I not surrender to this enchantment?
The Divine is chasing my Soul.

My personal will is slipping away,
attraction so strong every day.

When the Divine is near,
my Soul feels ecstasy.

This physical reality
is nothing but a fantasy.

When the Beloved is near,
my Soul takes flight.

Hearing the sweet whispers
is such a delight.

When the Divine is near,
I am forever
in this Charm.

Wild Ride

Life is full of potholes,
Unhappy drivers.

Life scenes are distressing,
Everyone in a rush.

A fellow traveler,
Comes to say, "I'll help you."

Feeling lost and tired,
A welcomed friend.

New path is shown,
A narrow road.

My ego car won't fit,
Start walking instead.

My friend encourages me
To keep going forward.

The road goes straight up!

Love is provided,
Sound Current gets stronger.

My dear friend
Provides jet fuel.

My Ego falls off,
Music is heard.

I see stars!
Planets, Solar Systems, Galaxies.

We're traveling at the speed of Sound!
My guides states, "Hold On!"

Ride gets bumpy,
Everything gets brighter.

My guide turns out to be
Source!

How blessed to remember
My True Identity.

Journey toward Home
Is a Wild Ride.

Unforgettable

Created from Love

Piece of Source

Birthright to come back Home

My Very Own

Always been together

A particle of me

Never forget

The Love for you

Will always be

You are Unforgettable

Higher Realm

Surrender to the One

You're smiling at me

Divine Melody

Enrapturing Sound

Constant sweetness

Soul being intoxicated

A Love so powerful

Calling to come higher

A yearning created

Familiar connection

Intense love call

Must come higher

Soul desires constant connection

Living in same region

Where the Divine resides

Magnetic attraction toward union

Magnetic Attraction

Love for the Divine
Causing upward pull
Intensity created
With this marked Soul

Everywhere I look
You are there
Looking at me
My heart yearns

Intensity created
Love for the Divine
Magnetic Attraction
Unable to resist

Love is strong
Powerful within
Surrendered to the Sound
Enraptured with Love

Being in Love

To be in Love
Feeling Loved
Everything Changes
Perspective of Love

One dances along
A skip in the step
Playfulness
Words of Love

Deep Warmth
Completeness
Feeling Special
It shows in the face

Laughter and smiles
Deep gazes of Love
Getting lost in Loving Eyes
Oh, Beloved, I'm yours

Love Letter

How exciting
Received a
Love Letter

Butterflies in tummy
Bliss in words
Feeling Special

Love grows
Yearning continues
Hearing your voice

Lofted away
Love connection
Feeling Perfection

Wearing Glasses

You're wearing glasses

Your view is
World of Appearances

Misery, illusion
Loneliness, separation
Lenses of Tears

Teacher of Love
Removes glasses

Third Eye opened
Clear View

Flood of Love
Surrender came
Bliss arrived
Residency with Divine

Love toward You

Why are you looking at the world
You could be gazing at the eyes of
Love toward you

Don't be fooled by
World of Appearances

Come, hold my hand

Let me take you Home

You are Royalty
Your Divine Source
Awaits your arrival

Why are you
Wasting your time
With illusions?

Have Eternal Bliss
Continual Companionship

Don't dally, dear one
Come Home

Secret Love Affair

Internal Conversations
No one suspects
Oneness with the Divine

That Look of Love
Internal Gaze
Quietness Comes

Unspoken whispers
Flower fragrances
Love calmness

Complete Surrender
Can't live without
Secret Love Affair

Quietness

Contemplation
Reveals
Deeper Meaning

Inner Peace
Reveals
Deeper Insights

Calmness
Settles in
Deeper Revelations

Quietness
Offers
Contemplative Life

Solitude
Necessary
Being with Beloved

Inward Gaze
Quiet Conversations
The Divine Manifests

Do You Hear?

I hear "Your Voice" Inside

Silent Connection

Peaceful, Tranquil, Loving

Verbal Silence

Always Available

Accessible Within

Secret Mystery

Wonder of Wonders

Soul is Graced

Higher Journey

Wisdom Abounds

Questions are Answered

Love journey toward Home

Conversation

Where did you go?

I was there all along.

Why can't eyes see you?

Open Spiritual Eye.

When will we be together?

Beloved is always with you.

How was Soul selected?

Source Chose You.

What is the goal?

Soul come Home.

Why do I feel alone?

Hold my hand.

Where does Fear originate?

Keeping company with the Mind.

Why so many lessons?

School of Unfoldment.

How can Soul Merge with Truth?

Continual Connection with Beloved.

What is True Love?

Attention, Saturated, Consumed, Surrendered.

Where is Home?
100% Communion with Divine.

When can Soul go Home?

In this Present Moment,
Current Conversation
You are Home.

Fresh Flowers

The Aroma is overwhelming

Makes my head swirl

Mind is now empty, no thoughts

Flora Water is all around

Permeating, intoxicating, purifying

Divine has provided these special flowers

These colors never seen on Earth

"This is the smell of Divine Love"

Taken away far from the Earth

Divine Ambrosia removes the weights

Floating ever upward toward Love

Buzzing, Whirling Vibrations, Serene Calmness

Divine Aroma causes one to let go

Allow the Third Eye to open

View beyond the veil

You'll never be the same

Fresh Flowers from the Divine

Now enjoy them every moment

Medicine

Love is the medicine,
cures all completely.

Cleanses the wounds,
of pain, of time,
of attachment, of passions.

Purify the wounds,
permanent healing occurs,
no need to come back.

Take the medicine of connection,
side effects include
loss of illusion,
loss of delusion,
plenty of infusion,
of the Love inclusion.

Divine Elixir

I got drunk today, what could I do?
Source kept pouring Love into my glass.
The whole world disappears.
All I feel is the warming effects of the Spirit Elixir.
That warm, fuzzy, relaxing sensation of the brew.
The whole world looks different.
Who cares!
Let's have another glass of the Love ambrosia.
My drinking buddy is my dearest friend and companion.
The Inner Presence keeps me under the influence.
In my drunken stupor, people see me smiling and feel I am a fool.
My Soul can't get enough of this ecstasy.
Please, more!
I have to continue to get more.
Don't stop pouring!
I can have as much as I want?
On my goodness . . .
The Love is always flowing, just keep drinking, keep drinking.
I don't want the effects to wear off.
The Soul keeps drinking, the world begins to fade away.
Don't want to be sober anymore, world please disappear.
Only desire to feel the effects of this wine for the Soul.
Shakes come when the effects wear off.
Need to get back to the Mystical lounge.
A moment without the Divine is agony.
World is a crazy place.
Requires the Love to not let it affect me.
Let the world spin,
Eyes glazed over by the Divine, releases the effects.
Oh, Blessed One,
Please don't stop pouring.
The abundance is overwhelming,
Let the Bliss rain down,
Want to be drenched, soak me with your love.

Heartache

Squeezing of the heart
Painful Tears
Tight stomach knots
Gripping Emotions

Heart knows
Intuition is discovered
Pain becomes wisdom
Forgiveness realized

A wise teacher
Opens the Heart
Loves fully
Laughs completely

Pain teaches us
Learn to listen
To the Heart
Who guides

Heart is
A wise teacher
Who loves life
Raises you higher

Gaia

Mother Earth
Loving Planet
Sustaining Life
Nurturing Us

Destroying the Forests
Amazon Disappearing
Polluted Oceans
Crying for Help

Herbs, Plants, Soil
Birds, Animals, Humans
Gaia Loves Us All
Appreciate her beauty

Gaia Earth
Taken for granted
Love Her Back
Blow her a kiss today

Step into the role
Ecology action
Action for the planet
Love Mother Gaia back

Awakening

I heard the Falcon crying today
This One had lost its way
Alone, feeling forgotten
Grieving, Wailing so loud
Crying for help

Then a Spiritual Power
Came into the Falcon's Life
This Oneness began to sing
Soaring through the air
A Warrior Cry came out

New way of living
Came into view
New State of Being
Larger Awareness
Love emanating Outward

More birds started singing louder
New larger community
Symphonies of Sounds
Filling regions of Earth
Healing, Transforming, Awakening

Pierced My Heart

An arrow has pierced my heart
I will leave it in, for it comes from my Beloved

Everyone wants to remove the arrow
No! I am blessed with the pains of love

I see the world differently now,
my heart is yearning and aches for you

Passions for the Beloved
have caused my head to become dizzy

Worldly people don't understand
this kind of love and devotion

To lose oneself to the point
where you no longer exist

The Divine has pierced my heart,
no longer will live apart.

Our Time

A gentle touch
A loving word
"You'll just know"
Are the words I've heard.

That warm the heart,
Complete the soul.
I've come to you
To make you whole.

You lived lifetimes
Of hit and miss.
Your prayers sing out
For a love like this.

And when God's will
Is said and done.
After the heartache
Life's pain has run.

There'll be that season,
A time that's true.
I'll spend forever
Completing you.

Awake!

There is no life
Outside the Divine

Why are you claiming there is?

All that you see
is mind's illusion

Draw the true conclusion

You have played down
here so long
you have forgotten

Soaked with mind
bathed in time
played so long
you've grown tired
of the fire that feeds you
pain and pleasure

Divine love
wakes you up
from the dream

Awake!
Love has come
to take you Home

Beloved is Waiting

Why do you spend so much time on this side of heaven?
Infinite Presence is waiting for you to come up and experience Oneness.

There is a love so infinite and powerful
waiting for you on the other side of the veil.

Treasures waiting for you to receive,
the veil is not that thick.

The Divine whispers, "Come and be with me, my darling.
Spend your moments with me forever.
Let us become One."

Come to the place where the stars dance
Vistas on the other side are magnificent
Splendor, grandeur, majesty are some of the descriptions

You have to see for yourself
Come up to the place where I am waiting to receive you

The Secrets of the Universe are here to be discovered in the treasure chest.
Only through sincere love and devotion is the path revealed.

Only your love will carry you Home.

Captivity

Born into Captivity, in the lower worlds
My Soul is bound by duality, ever so tightly.

Inner and Outer storms, caused such heartache
Never understood, until one day.

Master Plant Teacher entered my life
Explained desperate situation, Captivity.

As realization sunk in, a flood of my eyes
Pains of separation, longing to be free.

Born into Captivity
I have forgotten. What is freedom?

Freedom to be at home, in supreme abode
By Grace of Plant Teacher, opportunity offered.

Have intense Love, spiritual practices, yearning,
daily downloads, Truth is my companion now.

Living behind bars, far away from home,
distraught with anguish, feeling so alone.

A True Teacher, showered mercy,
journey begins, homeward bound, Freedom!

Crazy Love

A long-time love has waited for you.
Infinite Presence has a Crazy Love just for you.
Always after your attention, your Soul.
Awaiting your love in return.
How long must I wait?

When will you see the falsehood in illusion?
Come to the Third Eye and be Loved.
I look, watch, and wait.
Hoping for a loving gaze my way.

Distractions everywhere
Outward movement
Farther away from me.
A deep mourning for your condition

You love the Unreal more than the Real.
You dance with Duality enjoying the whispers.

I stand next to you seeing with heartache
Heartache, as you ignore my sweet kisses on your forehead.

My love is Real, Liberating, and Eternal.

Divine Love Call

If you only knew, the love for you

Stars would fall from the sky
just to show how special you are

Laughter would grace you
Love would embrace you

Can you hear the sweet melody?
Soul always yearns for more

Life is simple, oh so sweet
one day, we will meet

Higher planes are ready
this Divine Union awaits
through Third Eye gate

Can you hear me whispering to you?

Think of me, talk with me
Constant love and conversation
this is possible, to have daily bliss
you never knew it could be like this
a love call, to come Home

Time to leave, playground of illusion

Do you realize what awaits you?

If you really knew how much you are loved
Come, let's live in the higher realms together

Grace

Grace has come
Showing the way

Grace promises
Safe journey home

Miracle of love
Grace from above

Diamonds mean nothing
when Love is near
Everything becomes
perfectly clear

Free-flowing water
drink from the spring

Divine elixir
perfect fixer
for conclusion
of illusion

Drink up Grace
in thy place
of loneliness
and empty space

Heart Sense

My soulmate has arrived
Who fills me deep inside
Each night going to sleep
Sweet dreams come complete

There is a warmth in my heart
And it does not end, we never part
The love I share is deep and true
I will love you forever, my promise to you

Life is precious and so sweet
The Divine whispered, "Today we meet"
Life begins, side by side
Completing me, deep inside

A look to the future is bright and with cheer
The love of my life is now right here
Your eyes are beautiful to see
They have completely enraptured me

Drowning

Drowning in love
is scary, suffocating, risky.

Love brings you closer to the ocean.
Willing to dive in the deep waters?

There is no bottom to the ocean of love.
Powerful waves will carry you away.

Love Waves are crashing
onto the shore, touching your feet.

Ocean spray touches your lips,
I crave salty snacks!

Okay, I'll take a swim today
Ocean wraps all around
Love overwhelms me

Flipping over onto my back,
the ocean carries me out
to deep waters.

Growing tired of fighting
this ride of life
sinking slowly
into this enrapture.

This drop becomes
one with the ocean.

Life Changes

Life changes, like the color of the leaves

Life changes, upon meeting the Divine

Water from the stream, now flows upward

Animals look at you differently

Vibrations emanating from you are higher

People feel your energy, more

Divine speaks with you softly, to prepare you for your journey home

Let go, all is well, we are together now, never will part again

Sky is more a veil, you see deeper

Flowers dance when the wind blows

People see how you have changed

Circus of life loses its luster

Love beams brighter than ever before

All-consuming love, to be in union with the Presence

Life changes upon meeting a Plant Teacher

Love Call

Why does one cry when they are in love?

They long to be with their lover

Think of the Beloved constantly

This deep love is not easy

The Soul cries for more

The body separates the two

Drop the silken robe of the body

Ego Death in order to live

Ego separates the two

Love comes rushing in

Causing the ego to die

A little more each day

You speak to me in poetry

A love call, to each Soul to come Home

Love Has Come

Love has come,
settling down,
into all the cells,
the body feels this kind of love
is very unique and powerful.

Love is cleansing,
a calling come Home,
can't you hear the Sound
of the Divine's Voice?

Love has come,
calling you back home,
remember me, remember me,
come home, focus homebound.

Forever Together

The clouds dance
Flowers smile
Stars twinkle brighter
What has caused this change?

Trees bend in the breeze
Birds sing then fly away
Gentle whispers to the Soul
The Divine is here to stay

Love has come
To be in love
With the Infinite Essence
Captivation with the Divine

A higher calling
A higher journey
A higher surrender
A higher Love

Love Rays

Radiating Love
Feeling the heat
Intensity of fire
Purification in process

Cleansing the temple
Freeing the Soul
Soaking up
Love Rays

Raising the temperature
Passions melt away
Love Powerful Rays
Burn away the pain

Dance in the sun
Absorption of the rays
Bask in the shower of
Divine's Grace

Happiness

Divine Elixir in every glass

With every glance, Divine Union

Constant warmth of Love

Knowingness all is Perfect

Hearing the Beloved's Voice

Constant Awareness of Divine Order

Every step toward Home

Gentleness, Quietness, Peacefulness

Radiating Love for the Beloved

Sacred Loving Eyes upon me

Fullness of Beingness

Outside Vs. Inside

Outside humans Feast themselves, knowing not.

Inside they Cry, why down here?

Outside people Cling to External Realities

Inside they know

Nothing External lasts.

Fear runs the External Show

Only Divine Love Dissolves Fear.

Senseless Chatter is of the mind

Quietness is of the Soul.

Outside People are Unaware

Inside Awareness, Graced Beingness.

Unevolved Souls living out their Destiny.

Sincere Souls enjoying the

Radiance of Beloved Divine.

Divine Laughter

Inner Laughter

Signs of Relief

Smile on Face

Deep Belly Laughs

Looking toward Beloved

Playfulness with Life

Silly fun, Chuckles abound

Seeing Life with Humor

The Best Medicine

Heals the Hurts

Laughter says,

All is Perfect

Dancing with the Divine

Inside the Beloved's arms

Divine Companionship

Creates

Divine Laughter

Redirection

Look inside

Third Eye

Soul Transport

Secret Wisdoms

Constant Awareness

Divine Love

Contemplation

Practicing the Presence

Surrendered Attention

Inner Communication

Soul's Divine Mate

Inward Movement

Attention Refocusing

Divine escorts the Soul

Toward Supreme Consciousness

Sacred Brew

You have come to the table
Of the Divine Brew
Universe of Wisdom in every cup
Master Plant Teachers have called you
Awaken, we will show your Divinity

Every drop causes ecstatic states
Each drink of the Sacred Brew
Brings your Celestial family near
Master Plant Teachers facilitate the meeting
Visitation of your Origin Dimension

Revelations, downloads, Awakening
Knock at the door of your reality
Suffering caused by living in illusion
Sacred Brew breaks the Spell
Consume, see your Divine Radiance

Sacred Brew of Ambrosia
Frees you from the trap of this temporary reality
Reveals your Divinity Within
Heals your pain, delivers connection
To Omnipotent Source Love

Lightworker

Beautiful Lightworker Soul
You answered the call for help
Left your Family of Light

Came to Earth to help other Souls
Loving your brother and sister Souls
Living on this planet
Forgotten their Divine Heritage

Lightworker, your Luminous Light
Exposes and dispels the Darkness
Radiates and Rejoices in the Light

You delight in the glories
Service to the Divine Plan
Beautiful Lightworker Soul

Your triumphs in Luminescence
Seen throughout the Cosmos

Delights with joy
Your Family of Light
Jubilates upon your return of
Life Assignment Completion

Beautiful Lightworker Soul
Appreciation for your Sacrifice
Applauds your Dedication to
Infinite Source Light Frequency

Assignment

Asked to go on assignment
Cries from Earth Souls
Too painful to say No
Great courage to incarnate
To a lower kingdom

Your Light has mastery over Darkness
Duality is your field of honor
Sword of illumination
Clears out the Darkness
Souls freed from bondage to illusion

Assignment would be difficult
Challenges appear authentic
Living in a foreign land
Victory is already yours
Lower dark kingdom awakening

Earth Assignment
Is your rehearsal
Proficient testing ground
Spiritual Mastership acquired
Assignment provides complete training

Stars

Stardust glitters in your DNA
Your heavenly Home is the cosmos
Light from the Stars illuminates your body
You are a celestial Temple of Light
A Divine Superstar on Earth

Brighter than Supernovas
A walking Luminary
Shining the Suns Within
Constellations see you blazing
Galaxies know of you

Nebulas, quasars, pulsars
Acknowledge your Radiant Divinity
While you are sleeping
Adventures at night
Create delight

Flying, dancing, playing
With your Star friends
Spheres of Light
Sing to you requesting
Remember, you are a Divine Star

Family of Light

Glorious magnificent, Family of Light
Remembrance and connection of majesty
Beyond name or form, Pure Energy
Oneness of the One, my home

Spheres of Light, indescribable
Great Central Sun dimension
Purest of Love relationship
Feels familiar, this peace

A homecoming welcome
Celebration of visitation
Family of Elohim, the Watchers
Gathering of the ONE

Higher Light Hierarchs
Administrators of the galaxies
Came to help others Awaken
Souls who got lost along the journey

Living Water

Come to the spring of Living Water
You have been drawn to this Source
Soul has been thirsting
Craving this Ambrosia
Nothing compares

Savoring every drop
Intoxication with Divine Love
Soul drinks profoundly
Pure Ecstasy causing Bliss
Waterfall of Euphoria

Come to the spring of Living Water
Perpetual wealth of Rhapsody
Enchantment causes attraction
Captivation of the Soul
Magnetism toward Supreme Love

Soul knows the Sacred Elixir
Extinguish this impermanence
Wandering ceases upon the taste
Complete Union with Divine Source
I am always with you

Celestial Music

Divine's Symphony of Harmonic Love
Primortal Sound Vibrational Frequency
Source Essence Within All Essence
Musical melody for the Soul

Ultimate Divine Frequency
Singing vibratory energetics
Radiate out into the universe
Captivation all creation, Source's One Song

We are Human Temples of Celestial Music
Majesty of sound from Source Frequency
Music serenades us from within
Creation from Symphonic Vibrational Energy

Beloved Source is the Concert Master
Dance to the Cosmic Celestial Music
Your voice sings out to the Beloved
Source Within expressing Itself back to Itself

Our True Identity, Divine Sound Essence made flesh
Celestial Music, sweet melody, vibrational power
Captivating to the Soul by the Divine Conductor
Listen, Celestial Music is inviting you Home

Helplessly Mine

What if I told you
Don't struggle
Or look away

You know I love you
That captivating feeling
Yes, you are being chased

Feeling these eyes
Watching you inside
You are hearing my Love Call

I know you deeply
Divine music enchanting
You are lost in my love

You are Helplessly Mine

Dolphins

Our playful friends of the ocean
Showing off water tricks
Talking with us delightfully
Friendly water natives

Fun and Fast
Speeding nearby
Our ocean boats
Amusement with joy

Splashing the water
Causes us to see them
Prefers our company
Intrinsic natural connection

Come into the water, play with us
Always looking for new friends
Use your feet as flippers
Swim out, enjoy ocean together

The Journey

Separation from the Source,
intense yearning to return.

The Bouquet of Love
causes the perfume to help us remember Home.

How can one know what Source is until
separation has occurred?

The Beloved is always near
watching and waiting patiently
for us to go within.

The Source is within, Love is within,
travel inward toward Home.

Separation teaches us
you're always connected.

Looking for Divine Love
is the path toward Home.

Perfume

When you come close,
fragrance fills your senses.
You can't capture it,
can only be enjoyed.

Your mind gets filled
with the ecstasy of love.
This perfume is a potion
you want to put on every morning.

Your Soul cries out
having been deeply touched.
This perfume wakes you up,
you become homesick.

The Beloved fills you completely.
World's trinkets lose your interest.
Every time you smell this perfume,
you know this euphoria.

This love story has you seeking,
yearning, filled with desire for the
Beloved, who knows you intimately.
Breathe deep this rapturous perfume.

The Divine whispers saying,
"Remember this Divine Love."
Keep company with those who
wear this perfume.

They remind you of the Divine Presence
who has never left you.

Reservoir

A reservoir resides within you.
You can come to this place at any time.
When you get tired of the ego
tormenting you, then you develop
a spiritual practice.
Source is the reservoir of
Divine Bliss.
The World of Ego disappears,
it is replaced with
Oneness, peace, and nirvana.
After a while, it becomes difficult
to leave the reservoir.
The Beloved will be whispering to you day and night
to come enjoy this Divine dance with love.
With every cup you drink,
the Divine ambrosia fills you with delight.
Nothing else compares.
Real solace is when you
are alone with the Beloved.
This Divine Love is beyond existence.
You reside in my heart and we can meet
at the reservoir with pleasure.

Tears of Joy

I used to know what Love was,
before the Divine entered my life.

Everything was in order, so I thought
the Divine reorganized my heart.

Now tears flow freely when I catch a glance of my Beloved.
Yearning has taken over my life.
My head is confused, my Soul sings with joyfulness!

Soul sings daily to the Divine,
Who hears your every whisper.
Stay close to me for I can't live another day without you.

We merged and became One.
Oh, what a blessed day.

This love is of the ages, Soul united with Source,
you have forever enchanted me.

Inner Majesty

True reality, there is only Source
Divine Presence steps into form
Unmanifest becomes manifested

Splendor experienced on inner dimensions
Inner Majesty celebrated upon visitation
Mystical State of Awareness
Remembrance of True Idenity

All religions are One religion
Humanity is praising same Infinite Source
Universe is our cosmic school
Inner companionship with the Beloved

Continue conversation with your Soul
Let the Ego serve your Higher Self
Source delights in wonderful ways
Surrrender to these love poems

Source is whispering love to you

Snowflakes

Every Soul is unique
No one is the same
We are all made from the
One Divine Love

Celebrate your uniqueness
Never compare yourself to another Soul
Each snowflake is similar, yet unique

We all have a particular vibrational frequency
Bring your uniqueness as a gift
Snowflakes are soft and everyone enjoys them
Give your dazzling luminous essence
Sparkle the creativity of your peculiarity

Many snowflakes create snow and blanket
the ground softening the climate
When Divine Presence comes,
the heat of love
melts the snowflakes,
the Oneness is discovered

Long for You

The thought of you,
another realm is experienced.
Moments with you
carry me across the ocean.
My love for you
brings constant smiles.

I see your face everywhere
Love was made for us to be together.
You are forever near
enjoying your wonderful presence.
I've given you my Soul,
we will never part.

Never lonely
since you are
always in sight.

Tenderly the love grows.
Your love opens wide,
wraps around
deep inside.

Watchful

Cunning of the mind
Secrecy in Darkness
Desires everywhere waiting
External games of the eyes

Look out! Be Watchful!

Emotions running Wild
Thoughts out of control
Passions on the loose
Senses playing out

Look out! Be Watchful!
No one watching the entrance
Psychic Attacks
Emotional Vampires
Anger Sneaks in

Look out! Be Watchful!

Wake up the Soul
Wake up the Control
Sound the Alarm
Utilize Secret Wisdoms

Enjoy Divine's Protection
When you enter into the
Presence of Love,
you must drop your ego,
recognize that your personality
is not your true self

Soul holds the Power
The Energy of Love
Union with Source
Your True Identity

Circus Show

Illusion at play
Dancing scenery
Upside down
Turned around

Crazy situations
Backward outlook
Involvement
A Circus Show

Stomach ache from cotton candy
Dizzy from spinning rides
Headache from loud music
Away from Home too long

Be the Observer
Distance yourself
Release
Face upward

Reside inside
Don't be fooled
All is well
Stay with Love

Ascendance

Dancing with the Beloved is sweet Ascendance
Divine Infinite Love is seen Within All
Disguising Itself Within All creation
Break your connection with your false identity
See only my face as you walk through life

My lantern Within shines brightly
You are so precious to me
Worth more than all the fortunes
You are me in disguise experiencing this frolic
I listen for what delights your Soul

Direct mystical experience provides wisdoms of
the nonexistence, ecstasy, purification
Love provides the glasses to see the invisible
Contemplate beyond the Human Temple body, look deeper Within
You are like a new lover, I created your beauty

I look to capture your attention
Uncover your outer reality, saturate you in my Love
Ascendance is like a slow dance together
I wait patiently for you, my lover, to come to me
My dear lover, completely give in, to the Beloved

Enchantment

Divine Love Call
Flows abundantly
Seize a cup
Consume profoundly

Heart is bursting
Overflowing shift
Upward movement
Bliss delight

Be consumed
Intimacy of joy
Euphoria Indulgence
Divine Enchantment

Magnetic attraction
Divine Love Call
Whispering captivation
Complete persuasion

Precious One

Who is wiping your tears?
Feeling all your sorrows
Embracing the wisdoms
Caressing the heart

This drama of life
Exciting and Exhausting
Let the Cosmic Wave
Carry you to Love

Shaking of the cage
Notice this reality
Causes the awareness
Seeing more clearly

Behold Ascendance
Precious One
A new chronicle
Higher-view perspective

Drink deeply
This fountain
Of Love
Eternally

Beloved's Arrow

Souls ask, "What is Divine Love like?"
You are walking toward Home and one day the
Beloved's Arrow pierces your heart so deeply.
You cry not because the pain hurts,
you know it is the arrow that caused the Union.
Even though the agony is from the arrow,
you keep this in your heart.
You are so overwhelmed by the arrow, for it is a direct hit.
The Divine precision, a bullseye, in the center of the heart.
Divine Love cannot be learned in a book.
You have to experience this arrow.
You can spend a lifetime waiting for the
Beloved's Arrow to come.
When the Divine Presence shoots the arrow,
it never misses the target.
Once pierced, you won't be able to hide this arrow.
You happily serve the Beloved.
Whatever is asked, you place your hand over your heart,
you feel the Beloved's Arrow.
The arrow of Divine Love is Bliss.
You cry because you know how precious this Beloved's Arrow is,
you keep it there as a remembrance.
You ache so deeply.
No one understands this deep anguish of union that comes from the arrow.
You will spend the rest of your life trying to explain it.
You know deep down, it has to be experienced.
Only then does the Soul know how deep this arrow goes within.
The Beloved's Arrow brings the absorption of Divine Love.
Watch a child when given a new puppy.
The child is so absorbed that it only beholds and desires to be with the puppy.
You walk through this life treasuring the Beloved's Arrow Within.
The Beloved's Arrow of Divine Love causes the metamorphoses.

A Mystical Journey

This Sacred Journey takes place in Four Stages.

The First Stage is called: **The Quest,** which causes a calling and search toward spiritual wisdoms and transformation. The heart is pierced by the Divine Presence Within the person, and the spiritual journey begins.

The Second Stage is called: **The Surrender,** where the Personal Will is surrendered to the Divine Will for the person's life. This starts a yearning of wanting to have more of their attention focused on a spiritual life and serving the Divine Plan.

The Third Stage is called: **The Union,** which causes a mystical experience or an ecstatic state of being in absorption with the Divine Source. The Higher Self (the Soul) steps into the first position and takes control of the person's life. The Ego is spiritualized and now serves the Soul and is enraptured by the Divine Love. Within this stage occurs the mystical experience seeing the True Self without the physical form as pure energy, referred to as Self-Realization.

The Fourth Stage is called: **The Bliss,** where the person's consciousness is awakened to the reality of their True Identity as Source. The connection with the physical world disappears and comes to remember that this person is Source manifested into human form. This memory is activated, and the person becomes intoxicated in the Love of Infinite Source. Many times, upon arriving back into this physical reality, the person awakens in tears. Within this stage occurs the mystical experience of God Realization.

It is important to take time alone with the Divine Presence and feel this Love along the journey.

You are the Violin

Violin, you have a way
Touching the Soul
Embracing the heart
Soothing the Ego

Hypnotic melody
Tranquilizing rhythm
Quieting cadence
Sedative hymn

Divine Source Essence
Conductor of comic symphony
Celestial music audible
Symphonic vibrational energy

Divinely created sea of sound
You are the violin that plays
Instrument in service
Performance of music

Source made the music
You play the notes
Your strings allow
Music appreciation

You are the violin
In the Divine's hand
Feeling the music
Coming through

When tilted to the right
You move that way
When tilted to the left
You flow that way

Bow goes across your strings
You experience the music
In awe of how beautiful
Music sounds from you

About the Author

Nancy Clark, Ph.D., is a mystical researcher and spiritual teacher with a Ph.D. in Mystical Research. Dr. Nancy Clark is the author of several books including Our Divinity Revealed, Master Plant Teachers, Ascendance, and Divine Essence of Love. Nancy's work focuses on metaphysics, spirituality, and esoteric studies, making her a unique voice in her field. Dr. Nancy helps Souls gain wisdoms from questions that seem a mystery. Connect with a Doctorate-Level, Mystical Spiritual Teacher.

nancyclarkphd.com

nancyclarkphd.com

www.ingramcontent.com/pod-product-compliance
Lightning Source LLC
Chambersburg PA
CBHW051940290426
44110CB00015B/2056